TWAYNE'S WORLD AUTHORS SERIES
A Survey of the World's Literature

Sylvia Bowman, Indiana University
GENERAL EDITOR

SPAIN

Gerald Wade, Vanderbilt University
EDITOR

Don Juan Manuel

(TWAS 303)

TWAYNE'S WORLD AUTHORS SERIES (TWAS)

*The purpose of TWAS is to survey the major writers
—novelists, dramatists, historians, poets, philosophers,
and critics—of the nations of the world. Among the
national literatures covered are those of Australia,
Canada, China, Eastern Europe, France, Germany,
Greece, India, Italy, Japan, Latin America, the Neth-
erlands, New Zealand, Poland, Russia, Scandinavia,
Spain, and the African nations, as well as Hebrew,
Yiddish, and Latin Classical literatures. This survey
is complemented by Twayne's United States Authors
Series and English Authors Series.*

*The intent of each volume in these series is to present
a critical-analytical study of the works of the writer;
to include biographical and historical material that
may be necessary for understanding, appreciation,
and critical appraisal of the writer; and to present all
material in clear, concise English—but not to vitiate
the scholarly content of the work by doing so.*

Don Juan Manuel

By H. Tracy Sturcken

Pennsylvania State University

Twayne Publishers, Inc. :: New York

Library of Congress Cataloging in Publication Data

Sturcken, H Tracy.
  Don Juan Manuel.

  (Twayne's world authors series, TWAS 303. Spain)
  Bibliography: p.
  1.   Juan Manuel, Prince of Castile, 1282–1348.
I.   Title.
PQ6402.S8   863'.1   73–15586
ISBN 0–8057–2590–3

To those pleasant afternoons
with the old man of Arlanza
who still sits in the ruins
recalling the earth-trembling charge
of the men of Fernán González

Et así contesçe en [. . .] las scripturas:
toman de lo que fallan en un lugar et
acuerdan en lo que fallan en otros lugares
et de todo fazen una razón; et así fiz yo
de lo que oý a muchas personas que eran
muy crederas [. . .] Et vos et los que
este scripto leyeren, si lo quisiéredes
crer, plazer nos a; et si fallaredes otra
razón mejor que ésta, a mí me plazerá más
que la falledes et que la creades.
—Libro de las armas [prologue]

Preface

Don Juan Manuel's substantial reputation in medieval Spanish literature has been acquired, quite properly, on the basis of his major contribution to the evolution of prose fiction on the peninsula. He could also be placed among those Spanish authors most frequently read, if this judgment is based solely on a few select tales from *El Conde Lucanor* (*Count Lucanor*). The recognition given his remaining seven works has been somewhat scant, and one is left with the impression that they have gone largely unread over the years. Yet few figures in early Spanish literature tell us more of themselves and the Spain they lived in, with the totality of their written work, than does Juan Manuel.

The major role played by this writer in early fourteenth-century Castilian and Aragonese history and his participation in many of the decisive events of that period obviously cannot be ignored. It has been necessary, in this general introduction to the man and what he has to say, to take up in some detail his place in the turbulent and uneasy Castile of his day; without such a perspective, Juan Manuel's ideas and art are often imperfectly understood. The longest section of this study is naturally devoted to his most creative effort, a collection of short tales. I have arbitrarily grouped his other works in two short chapters without regard for their purported chronology; the reasons will be clear as they are taken up.

I have used freely the work of many writers who have had something to say about Don Juan Manuel, and trust that my sources have been duly indicated. If I have failed to do so at some point, it has not been intentional. The texts I quote are from the first edition of said texts listed under Primary Sources in the Bibliography; occasional page references are likewise to those editions. Translations are mine. I wish to thank the Liberal

Arts Research Office of the Pennsylvania State University for a grant that made a part of the research for this book possible.

H. TRACY STURCKEN

University Park, Pennsylvania

Contents

Chronology

1282   May 5: Don Juan Manuel born in Escalona (Toledo).

1283   Christmas: Death of his father, the Infante Manuel.

1290   Death of his mother, Beatriz of Savoy.

1295   Don Juan Manuel meets a dying Sancho IV (d. April 25); Cerda adherents organize with plans to seize crown; minority of Fernando IV initiates period of political unrest and occasional armed conflict in Castile persisting through minority of Alfonso XI.

1296   Aragon begins seizure of Alicante area in the frontier domain of Murcia, governed by Don Juan as Adelantado.

1299   Don Juan Manuel marries Infanta Isabel of Mallorca (d. 1301).

1300   Don Juan importunes María de Molina, acquiring Alarcón in lieu of Elche territories taken by Aragonese.

1303   May 9: Játiva meeting of Don Juan Manuel and Jaime II of Aragon; paper marriage to Infanta Constanza; Elche, etc., revert to Don Juan.

1304   Castilian-Aragonese pact ending eight-year Murcia dispute signed at meeting between Agreda and Tarazona; Aragon retains area represented by modern Alicante.

1305   Don Juan gives up Alarcón (to Castile) for Cartagena (from Aragon).

1306   May: Marital contract finalized in Valencia; consumptive Constanza, 6, taken to castle in Villena.

1309   Castilian-Aragonese pact at Alcalá to attack Granada; Don Juan Manuel and Infante Juan desert field at Algeciras.

1312   April 3: Don Juan marries Constanza of Aragon in Játiva; their two children who live to adulthood are Constanza and Beatriz. September 9: Sudden death of tubercular Fernando IV; future Alfonso XI thirteen months old.

1313   Threat of civil war as turbulent minority of Alfonso XI begins; Infantes Juan and Pedro, and María de Molina, act as regents independently, as Cortes stipulate; Don Juan Manuel is appointed *mayordomo* (comptroller) to crown.

1318   Don Juan founds Dominican house at Peñafiel.

1319   June 24–25: Regents' deaths in the Vega; general anarchy during crisis of 1319–1325; Infante Felipe, Juan el Tuerto, and Don Juan Manuel dispute regency.

1321   May: Severe confrontation begins between Don Juan Manuel and brother-in-law Juan, Archbishop of Toledo. June 30: Death of María de Molina. Rural Castile prostrate with pillaging and looting.

c. 1321– *Crónica abreviada (Outline History), Caza (Hunting),* and
c. 1327 *Cavallero et escudero (Knight and Apprentice-Knight)* completed by Don Juan.

1325   August 13: Alfonso XI's minority ends. September: Reconciliation between Don Juan Manuel and Archbishop after latter's long visit with sister at Garcimuñoz. November 28: Alfonso XI-Constanza Manuel marital contract agreed upon in Valladolid.

1326   Summer: Don Juan Manuel victorious over Moslems in Málaga. On All Saints Day: Alfonso XI begins brutal grip on internal situation by assassinating Juan el Tuerto in Toro.

1327   Alfonso XI plans marriage to Portuguese Infanta; Don Juan Manuel's daughter Constanza held as pawn in Toro; Don Juan formally casts off allegiance to Castile, seeks alliance with Moslem Granada; enduring animosity toward Alfonso XI commences; eventual open warfare at Huete and Escalona; Jaime de Jérica in Peñafiel to aid Don Juan Manuel. September: Death in Garcimuñoz of Don Juan's wife Constanza of tuberculosis. All Souls Day: Death in Barcelona of Jaime II of Aragon.

1329   Don Juan Manuel marries Blanca Núñez, daughter of Juana Núñez and the son of first Fernando de la Cerda; their two children will be Fernando and Juana.

c. 1330– *Libro de los estados (Plan of Society)* completed by Don
c. 1332 Juan.

1333   Spring: Conciliatory meetings of Alfonso XI, Don Juan Manuel, and Juan Núñez. August: Gibraltar falls to Muhammad IV of Granada and Moroccan army newly arrived on peninsula.

1334 Four-year Castile-Granada-Morocco truce permits arming for decisive encounter; Don Juan Manuel declares self nominal subject of Aragon; from latter receives title "Príncipe de Villena."

1335 *Count Lucanor* is finished by Don Juan.

1336 February: Marriage by proxy of Constanza Manuel and Pedro, heir to Portuguese crown. Alfonso XI withholds safe-conduct. Don Juan's daughter remains secluded in Aragon. July: Don Juan again publicly disavows homage to Castilian crown. Unsuccessful attempt by Don Juan Manuel to employ massive coalition of peninsular forces against Alfonso XI; latter victorious at Oporto, Badajoz, etc., encounters.

c. 1336– *Libro infinido* (*Unfinished Book*) probably written.
c. 1338

1337 Juana Núñez "Palomilla" arranges truce between Alfonso XI and Don Juan Manuel.

c. 1337– *Libro de las tres razones* (*Three Topics*) and *Prólogo*
c. 1342 *general* (*General Prologue*) completed by Don Juan.

1340 July: Pact of Sevilla: Portuguese stipulate return of Constanza to her father. August: Nuptial mass at union of Pedro and Constanza Manuel in Portugal; a maid to attend the latter will be Inés de Castro, bastard daughter of a Galician noble. October 30: Alfonso XI defeats Merinid army at the Salado in last great encounter of the Reconquest; Don Juan Manuel both praised and criticized for part in this battle.

c. 1340– *Tratado de la Asunción* (*Essay on the Assumption*) writ-
c. 1346 ten by Don Juan.

1344 March: Algeciras falls to Alfonso XI after two-year siege; Don Juan Manuel leads Christian contingent into town bearing Castilian coat of arms.

c. 1347– Bubonic plague reaches Gibraltar.
c. 1349

1348 June 13: Death of Don Juan Manuel this Friday.

1350 Good Friday: Alfonso XI dies of plague at siege of Gibraltar. Leonor de Guzmán arranges marriage of her son Enrique and Juana Manuel.

1369 March 23: Assassination of Pedro I in Montiel. Juana Manuel is Queen of Castile after Trastámara victory.

1379 July 25: Don Juan Manuel's grandson is crowned in Burgos and reigns as second Trastámara, Juan I.

CHAPTER 1

The Man and His Age: 1282–1312

I *The Early Years*

TODAY the ruins of the once formidable castle of Escalona stand high over a winding curve made by the Alberche river on its way south to join the Tagus. The structure, battered and burned out by the French in the War of Independence, appears to be slowly crumbling down the slope; some of its stone, as often happens, went to brace the portico rimming the Plaza Mayor in the town below, but enough remains in its great square keep to shelter the bats that arrive at dawn to putrefy the surroundings once enjoyed by the lords of Castile. Here, in Escalona, in the province of Toledo, on May 5, 1282, the wife of the Infante Manuel gave birth to a son, named Juan possibly since the feast to follow on the sixth was that of St. John before the Latin Gate; the date of his baptism is not known.[1] The father of the boy who would become known as Don Juan Manuel was the youngest son of the great warrior king of Castile, Fernando III, called el Santo. The young Juan became aware early of the circumstances of his family and birthright, and his proud nature would later lead him to believe that the political situation might not have degenerated so miserably in his lifetime had the succession fallen to the line of Manuel. The eldest son of San Fernando, heir to the throne, had been Alfonso X el Sabio (Juan Manuel's uncle), a major force in cultural activity in thirteenth-century Castile.[2]

In both his mother (Beatriz of Savoy) and paternal grandmother (Beatriz of Swabia) Don Juan had female antecedents who were non-Hispanic. Although it may be curiously suggested on occasion that this had some influence on his character, particularly in the case of his German grandmother, there is obviously nothing to support such a contention. Don Juan's mother was his father's second wife. By his first wife (Constanza, daughter of Jaime I of Aragon), Manuel had a son, Alfonso, who died at an early age, the primogeniture passing to Don Juan as the male heir to the house of Manuel; and a daughter, Violante, who would outlive her parents, only to suffer an apparently vicious death in 1306 at the hands of her husband, the Infante Alfonso of Portugal.[3] Both parents would die when Don Juan was still very young: his father in 1283, and his mother seven years later.

His father's principal property in Castile had been Peñafiel, on the Duratón as it approaches the Duero; it passed legally to Don Juan in 1285. His father's other properties, largely grants from the first-born Alfonso X, included the title Adelantado of Murcia; an *adelantado*, royally appointed, exercises full judicial powers in a given territory. The title to certain lands in the area of Elche will always be considered by Don Juan a Manueline right acquired by his father when these lands lay beyond the jurisdiction of any political authority; a title, therefore, requiring no oath of fealty to any sovereign, Castilian or Aragonese. It will be the basis for his contention that the first-born sons in the line of Manuel rank in status above other landed nobility, and the possessions themselves, always near the fluctuating Castilian-Aragonese border, will be a matter for dissension during a good part of his early life.

In the late spring of 1294, at the age of twelve, he is introduced to war, in a lifetime that is to be filled with conflict of one kind or another: "And on that Pentecost my men fought well under my banner, for they conquered a great warrior, Abenbucar Avençayen, of the lineage of Moroccan royalty, who had crossed the frontier at Vera with a thousand horsemen. And they left me behind in Murcia because of the danger and my youth" (*Armas* [*Coat of Arms*], p. 87).[4] Early in 1295, the young Juan had a meeting in Madrid with his dying cousin, Sancho IV el Bravo (the Fierce), that he would describe over forty years later in *Armas*, in some of the most vivid pages he wrote, as a moving, emotional experience. Sancho, the second-born, had come to the throne of Castile following a violent relationship with his father, Alfonso X. The first-born, Fernando de la Cerda, had died in battle while still a young man of twenty-five; his wife had already given him two sons, Alfonso and Fernando, who then became legitimate heirs. The existence of these children, the Infantes de la Cerda, their eventual aspirations to the throne, and the designs of those around them, would contribute to embroiling Castile in a period of internal unrest that would last through the reigns of Sancho IV (1284–1295) and Fernando IV (1295–1312), and well into the reign of Alfonso XI (1312–1350).[5]

II *The Minority of Fernando IV Begins; First Marriage; A Cerda Plot; Settlement in Murcia*

The next period in the life of Don Juan Manuel encompasses the activity surrounding the succession to the Castilian throne (Sancho's son, the future Fernando IV, was still a minor in 1295) and several years of political maneuvering on Don Juan's part to retain his rights to the Elche properties. It covers approximately the decade between 1295 and 1304, with the latter year witnessing the cessation of quarreling between Castile and Aragon over rights to the Murcian territories and the signing of pacts to divide the territory peacefully. The Infante Manuel from the first had backed his older brother Sancho's attempts to seize control of Castile; his son would follow suit, making enemies of the Infantes de la Cerda. Swept away as children to Aragon by their grandmother Violante, who apparently feared for their safety at the hands of her son Sancho, the Infantes Alfonso and Fernando had signed over all Castilian rights in Murcia to the Aragonese crown; Violante was Aragonese herself, daughter of Jaime I.

With Sancho dead and his widow, María de Molina, struggling to preserve the rights to the throne of their young son Fernando against the claims of the Cerda youth as well as against those of the Infante Juan (another son of Alfonso X and Sancho's brother, who had received certain vague promises in his father's will), the situation was so fluid that Aragonese troops, their monarch claiming the right via the Cerda, had little difficulty in crushing the Castilian post at Alicante in 1296 and moving on Elche. Don Juan, seeing the futility of attempting to hold off a siege at Elche, agreed despairingly to recognize the King of Aragon as the ultimate authority over these lands. Now angry over this loss, the young Juan and his coterie proceeded to the Castilian court in residence at Cuéllar to demand reparations for the loss of Elche. Even though Don Juan had neglected to take part in the ceremonies in Toledo proclaiming the regency of Fernando, María de Molina saw fit to grant him proprietary rights over

Alarcón, to last as long as the Aragonese held Elche. Despite the fact that he and his father had always sided with the position taken by Sancho IV, the young Juan's advisers had seen to it that he took no part in the troubled succession to the throne immediately following Sancho's death. Nor did Don Juan Manuel have anything to say, at this time, of the claims of the Cerda youth, now living in Calatayud, or of the claims of the Infante Juan.

The first of Don Juan Manuel's three marriages took place toward the end of 1299, a marriage arranged five years earlier by Sancho IV. Sancho had acted all along as guardian of his brother's orphaned children, with the close-knit relations in the households of Sancho and Manuel proudly mentioned by Juan Manuel in *Armas*. The bride was the Infanta Isabel of Mallorca, whose life was cut short late in 1301 as she and her nineteen-year-old husband were planning a trip to her homeland, where the seriously ill Infanta hoped to regain her health.

Don Juan now appeared to be acting very much on his own and following well-laid plans designed to stabilize and increase his holdings. Many examples of eager self-aggrandizement were present for him to imitate. An unstable crown sat on the head of the young Fernando IV, held there by the Queen Mother María de Molina, a woman beset with impossible demands from noblemen on all sides, including those of Juan Manuel, who importuned her for primogeniture possession of Alarcón and the right to be lord of Alcaraz and Huete during his lifetime. Although rejection followed these demands, the young heir to the Manueline name and fortune was eager to make his presence felt.

Now a major decision was reached by Don Juan Manuel, in which for the first time he would join a group of noblemen who opposed the Castilian crown. He desired above all to bring about the return of Elche, if possible, and to retain Alarcón and other lands in the southeast that lay dangerously within easy reach of the Aragonese. A party was formed of nobles, including Don Juan, who for one reason or another would throw their support to Alfonso de la Cerda, provided they were able to obtain the backing of the King of Aragon. This group was generally led by the Infante Enrique; [6] the Cerda prince, nervously observing the negotiations from Almazán in Soria, believed at this point that he would soon be king of Castile. Don Juan Manuel was selected to have a preliminary discussion with Jaime of Aragon. Don Juan had already on his own, however, requested a meeting with this king, to discuss events in Castile which, according to the message (Giménez Soler, p. 267), were of such a serious nature that they could not be put in writing. It seems likely that Don Juan was here acting in his self-interest which may or may not have coincided with the interests of the party to which he was nominally attached; he will brag in *Estados (Plan of Society)* I, 70, of his secret diplomatic coups. The meeting took place in Játiva in May, 1303, during the course of which Don Juan formally asked for the hand of Jaime's daughter, Constanza. According to the documents signed then and there (Giménez Soler, pp. 265–66), the marriage was to take place eight years later, but only if the necessary papal dispensation (because of consanguinity) were obtained within the next three years. If this were accomplished, Don Juan could then take the child to be raised under his protection if he wished. She would eventually live in Villena, a property designated as collateral to secure the agreement by Don Juan; castles and females both made suitable properties for bartering in the fourteenth century. In all of this, the uppermost thought in Don Juan's mind was to protect himself against future loss of property arising from his new position opposing Fernando IV. This betrothal had apparently been planned by him for some time, since the signing could not have taken place so suddenly.

The articles of agreement included these extraordinary measures: Jaime would protect Don Juan Manuel against his enemies, especially and specifically the King of Castile, but excluding the Kings of Mallorca and France and the Cerda princes; Don Juan would follow the King of Aragon against the latter's enemies, but excluding Castile, in which case Don Juan would remain neutral. Other clauses were unusually beneficial to Don Juan, and this can be explained only as astute bargaining on the part of Don Juan plus the fear in Jaime's mind of a possible allied attack on Aragon from Castile and Moslem Granada.

A general meeting of the entire Cerda-supporting group was held in San Esteban de Gormaz, and a major meeting with Jaime was planned for June 20, 1303, in Ariza. The wily old Enrique, uncle of both the Cerda boy and Juan Manuel, looked forward to rich rewards for all when the Cerda grandson of Alfonso el Sabio would replace Fernando on the throne. An agreement detrimental to Castile was signed at Ariza. The stipulations (Giménez Soler, pp. 280–82) stated that Alarcón would remain permanently in Juan Manuel's family.[7] Don Juan will be the only one of this pro-Cerda group who will be recompensed to his satisfaction, after an accord on Murcia is reached.

The Infante Enrique, now very sick, reached Roa on his way to attempt to bring the Queen Mother around to agreeing to the pact signed at Ariza by her son's enemies. In Roa in August, 1303, he died, at which point in the *Chronicle of Fernando IV* (Chap. XI) Don Juan Manuel is accused, unjustly or not, of finding his uncle *sin fabla* (unconscious), and thinking him dead, of stripping the Roa house of its possessions (*BAE*, 66, p. 132).[8] The Queen Mother, as weary as the others of the long period of hostilities begun in 1296, was ready to make peace with Aragon, even to the point of acceding to many of the Ariza demands. She would not, however, agree to the use of the title "king" by Alfonso de la Cerda, nor at that time would she agree to a marriage between her daughter and this older Cerda. Her son, Fernando IV, infuriated by Don Juan's promise of neutrality to Jaime in the event of a Castilian-Aragonese war, apparently ordered his murder at this time. Jaime II, hearing of these plans, saw fit to warn Don Juan (Giménez Soler, p. 292) in October, 1303, not to attend meetings with representatives of the Castilian royal family or to enter any area that could become a trap, a precaution similarly insisted on in *Estados* I, 62 and 70, and *Lucanor*, tale 12. Juan Manuel's family physician, entrusted at this point with confidential missions, also reported overhearing such threats in Toledo from an official of Fernando IV.

With the agreements reached in 1304 large areas of Murcia passed to Aragon, and the final decision on the border between Castile and Aragon was to be decided the following year by representatives of the two crowns. It may be indicative of Don Juan's persistence to note that on one occasion the line of demarcation was established along an irregular course around his property at Yecla in order that this land might remain his as well as within the limits of Castile. This was done "because they knew well the ways of Don Juan Manuel who always forced his king to satisfy his claims and who had shown in the case of Alarcón how troublesome he could be" (Giménez Soler, p. 316).

The area around Elche went to Aragon, but immediate threats from Don Juan eventually brought on a later stipulation in which he was mollified by receiving Cartagena from Aragon in exchange for the less impressive Alarcón.

III   *Marriage Preparations; The Rebellious Clan of Lara*

The powerful Lara family headed by Juan Núñez had expected Don Juan Manuel to marry Juana Núñez, the widow of the Infante Enrique, rumor having it that the aged Infante had been unable to consummate his marriage with Juana. (More than two decades later Juan Manuel's third wife will be the daughter of this Juana and the younger Cerda prince, and the girl who might have been his wife will become his mother-in-law.) Don Juan's refusal was cause for a brief armed clash between the two parties at the Cortes in Medina del Campo in 1305. At Brihuega later that year, in June, Don Juan accepted the gift of a falcon from his future father-in-law, Jaime II, responding with a warm letter of thanks (Giménez Soler, p. 318). A few days earlier he had written to Jaime's queen, Blanche of Anjou, recommending his personal jongleur, Arias Paes, who was going to the tournament festivities at Artal de Luna; any kindness shown him would be appreciated.

With the Papal dispensation in hand, Juan Manuel and Jaime proceeded toward further marriage plans in August, 1306. For reasons unknown, the parties appeared eager to finish this business: Jaime suggested in January (Giménez Soler, p. 327) that to hurry things along he was willing to meet Don Juan in a wild wooded area as if they were planning a small hunting party. The final marital agreements were reached promptly: The child Constanza, now six, would live in the alcázar at Villena, from which Don Juan swore not to remove her, taking this oath in the presence of the Bishop of Valencia. The dowry remained unchanged at five thousand *marcas*; earlier property stipulations and one related to the possibility of Don Juan's death remained intact. The ceremony would take place when Constanza was twelve, a normal marriageable age. The modern notion of adolescence did not exist in the fourteenth century: Boys became (were treated as) adults in their mid-teens; girls, a year or two earlier.

Difficulties were continuing between the crown and certain

landed barons or *ricos-omnes*, as the peninsula moved slowly along the path toward centralized, absolute monarchical power. Juan Núñez de Lara was especially prone to making trouble for Fernando IV, whom Jaime II encouraged to take firm control of his kingdom. Don Juan Manuel, still at odds with the Núñez family, began to carry out guerrilla thrusts on Núñez property from Cuenca, claiming that he was helping the King. Fernando meanwhile had laid siege to Juan Núñez in Aranda and for a time slowed the Lara rebellion. Don Juan was called from Cuenca to take part in the siege but, moving slowly, had only reached Atienza when Núñez capitulated. Hoping to receive some reward in Vizcaya from the Lara lands, he was disappointed. The Cortes at Valladolid in 1307 were torn with dissension between king and *ricos-omnes*. The apparently callous murder of Don Juan's half-sister Violante had taken place late in 1306 in Vide, between Medellín and the Portuguese frontier. There was never any doubt in Don Juan's mind that a murder had been committed, and the dreadful incident caused him to ask Fernando (Giménez Soler, p. 344) to act on the matter. The affair is not mentioned in the correspondence extant after 1307.

IV *The Disastrous Siege of Algeciras*

During the poorly planned sieges against the Moslem strongholds at Algeciras and Almería in 1309–1310, an event of capital importance occurred that brought widespread disrepute to the name of Castile and Castilian arms. Don Juan Manuel played a highly visible role in this miserable affair, and, although his name was to be cleared of wrongdoing after all the excuses and recriminations had been made, doubts lingered on in some minds. The decision at Alcalá by Jaime II and Fernando IV to attack the Moslems came after a long lull in the Reconquest; not since Sancho IV seized Tarifa in 1292 had there been a concerted large-scale movement by Christian forces. Occasional strikes for booty and harassment by the Moslems had been occurring across the no-man's land that ran along the fringes of Almería, Granada, and Málaga. An agreement at Ariza between the highest Aragonese and Castilian lords (including Juan Manuel and the Infante Juan) spelled out the rewards: Granada would go to Castile, and Almería to Aragon, plus more territory should Almería not constitute a sixth of the bloc of Moslem lands.

Enormously expensive preparations were undertaken, but from the beginning there were rumblings of dissatisfaction. To achieve harmony among his forces and build an army of experienced warriors, rather than the customary grab-bag, undisciplined *mesnadas,* Fernando dispersed large sums, including all royal income from Jaén and Córdoba, and made promises of territorial rights. Don Juan Manuel demanded and received confirmation (Giménez Soler, p. 361) of Castilian territory recovered in this attack, in return for land in Almería that Alfonso el Sabio had long ago promised his father in anticipation of the conquest of Granada. With everyone apparently satisfied, the war machine cranked up. Castile would strike the western flank at Algeciras; the Aragonese navy would send troops against Almería. The Infante Juan and Juan Núñez said that they would fight gloriously, even seeking a death that would atone for past sins (Giménez Soler, p. 364); Juan Manuel reserved harsh comment for those who, with conscience not honestly clear, rushed off to die in Andalusia (*Estados* I, 76). There were many in the Cortes in Madrid who believed jubilantly that the complete withdrawal of the Moor was at hand.

Not, however, Don Juan Manuel. At least there is reason to believe that he never had faith that the expedition would succeed. He began to fret early over the safety of Constanza and urged his father-in-law in Barcelona (Giménez Soler, pp. 374–75) that she be moved from Villena. He believed that Alarcón would provide greater safety, since a Moslem raiding party could reach Villena on a quick strike. The Aragonese King saw no immediate danger and did not want his daughter moved, even though Don Juan, in an effort to assure Jaime, offered to go through with the final ceremony but not consummate the marriage or even return to his wife's alcázar for two years.

Juan Manuel was probably more experienced than most of Fernando's officers in the tactics of the Moslems. The King appeared to favor advice, nevertheless, from the Lara and Haro families, giving them preferential consideration over the two Juans who now, it seemed, cared little for any campaign that would enhance the prestige of Fernando. Although they ostensibly went along with the battle plans, they must have already begun to grumble privately; Don Juan, for example, wished to lead the attack from Murcia, in his capacity as Adelantado, but instead was assigned by Fernando to serve as one of several leaders against Algeciras. The Infante Juan and the lord of Peña-fiel were not two who forgave easily or forgot past rancors.

Their decision to end abruptly their participation in the attack, deserting the remaining forces in the field, was called high treason by some (Giménez Soler, pp. 367–71, 383–84), and meant the certain failure of the expedition and the utter waste of huge expenditures of human and material resources. For a period correspondence between chancelleries dealt with little else. Explanations were demanded, especially by Jaime, who withdrew to his ships, as did Fernando to Sevilla. The Infante Juan's excuse later was that Fernando planned to kill him. Don Juan Manuel's explanation of his actions to Jaime included an order he claimed Fernando had given him to remain at the Infante's side in order to prevent the "rebel" Infante from committing acts dangerous to the crown; Don Juan also insisted that a quantity of money promised him by Fernando had never been received. It appeared that the Infante precipitated the rebellious action, and he would feel the brunt of the condemnation. Juan Manuel offered María de Molina as witness to the truth of his claims, but even after the affair finally ceased to be mentioned, a sour taste lingered on. For several months the two first cousins fell from sight, "wandering up and down the kingdom of León," the chronicles would say, for no reason other than their fear of reprisal for their desertion. In all of these claims, explanations, accusations, and counterclaims, there was probably a degree of truth. The most serious charge that probably should be made against Juan Manuel is that he went along with the war plans, yet never was willing to carry out fully what was expected of him; and at times his contentions, such as the one that he thought the war would entail only strike-and-destroy attacks and not laying siege to walled enclosures, were difficult to substantiate.

V *A Troubled Castile at the Death of Fernando IV*

The final years of Fernando IV can be characterized as unsettled, with the political turmoil due in no small measure to Fernando's lack of attention to matters of state. He was so addicted to sports and amusements that it was said (Giménez Soler, p. 393) he devoted inordinate amounts of time to these activities; he was also accused of constantly backing down on his word and giving in to the last person who had his ear. Yet the record of shifting loyalties for and against this physically as well as morally weak monarch by power-seeking barons also explains in large part the difficulties in bringing about peace in the land. Don Juan Manuel blamed much of the animosity he encountered from Castilian sources on his close relations with Jaime of Aragon. He complained bitterly to Jaime in a long letter (Giménez Soler, p. 377) that he was being accused falsely in Castilian circles concerning his activities at Algeciras. This harsh document in Catalan was followed by a firm response from the Aragonese king denying that there was ever any intent to impugn Don Juan's motives.

A sore point of contention with Don Juan was the planned marriage of the Aragonese Infanta María, another daughter of Jaime, into the Castilian royal family, thus lessening Don Juan's stature in Castile as the noble there who represented interests backed by the might of Aragon. María was to marry Pedro, Fernando's brother, and both royal courts moved quickly to agree on the dowries and patrimony to be granted, to the great displeasure of Juan Manuel. Fernando must have been eager to reach an accord, offering the future couple Santander and Medina de Ríoseco, as well as Viana in Navarra and towns along the Castilian border so that María might be near Aragonese territory. Jaime, having sought lands in eastern Soria and Guadalajara near Aragon as Pedro's patrimony, was eventually satisfied, and the plans moved to completion. The peevishness Don Juan felt at seeing his influence diminished was evident to all.

Political conditions in Castile disintegrated to the disaster point with the serious and, for a time, incapacitating illness of Fernando in 1310, and it would be a long and lugubrious tale indeed were all the self-aggrandizing activities of the nobles detailed at this point. Fernando was to recover from this illness (but not from the seizure that would end his life in 1312), and even see a son, the future Alfonso XI, born in August, 1311, thus greatly upsetting those relatives who had plans for dividing Castile among themselves should there be no heir. Don Juan Manuel detested Fernando's brother and cared little if it were known that he would do anything to prevent Pedro's assuming the crown. Jaime pleaded with his son-in-law not to act hastily and to respect the legal authority of the monarchy. This seems to have been the general course followed by Don Juan, despite his annoyance earlier in 1311 at a scandalous attempt in broad daylight by the King himself, his brother Pedro, and Núñez de Lara to murder the Infante Juan. Constantly in and out of the King's favor, and always loudly complaining of Fernando's intentions (usually with good reason), the Infante Juan, Sancho IV's younger brother and hence Fernando's uncle, had ridden out of Burgos, his usual residence, on a day in January, 1311, to set his hawk after two heron in the direction of Quintanadueñas. According to the Aragonese account (Giménez Soler, p. 385) sent by Jaime's informant, Guillén Palacín, a ringing bell signaled the pursuit to kill the Infante; another version of what happened is in the *Chronicle of Fernando IV*, Ch. 17 (*BAE*, 66). The Infante escaped to Villalón and was later joined in Becerril de Campos by Don Juan Manuel, who "slipped from Burgos at midnight and passed through Peñafiel to provision his men." Palacín's letter is sympathetic to the two Juans and explicitly accuses the King of an attempted murder; he promises to tell more in person later on because "the events here are extraordinary and too complicated to detail" (*los feytos estos son muy grandes e largos de escrivir*). This picture of a politically unsettled Castile should suffice.

Constanza of Aragon became Juan Manuel's v 'e in Játiva in April, 1312, in a ceremony blessed by the Bishop of Tortosa and witnessed by most of the Aragonese royal family. Constanza, now twelve, was accompanied by Doña Saurina, her governess, after the ceremony, because there is a letter in Catalan (Giménez Soler, p. 407) from Saurina to Jaime, written in Chinchilla a week after the wedding, that describes the newly-wed couple's happiness and the bride's delight with the arrival of bolts of gold and silver fabric from the Burgos mills. In July they settled in the castle at Garcimuñoz in Cuenca, where Don Juan would probably have preferred to live most of the year, for the abundance of game in the Júcar, Rus, and Záncara basins, and for its access to Aragon and Murcia, as well as the eastern approaches to Castile. They were still there in September when word came of the death of Fernando IV.

CHAPTER 2

The Man and His Age: 1312–1348

I   The Regency of Alfonso XI Begins

THE death of Fernando IV brought on no serious difficulties between Castile and Granada since the latter was torn by a series of internal revolts that would leave the Nasrid dynasty there unstable. Don Juan Manuel spent some time in Murcia in 1312, however, ready to repel any sudden assaults. The two principal aspirants to the regency were the Infante Juan (the minor Alfonso's great-uncle) and the Infante Pedro (the boy's uncle). The young Pedro's wife was an Aragonese Infanta, hence Juan Manuel's sister-in-law, and Pedro eagerly sought the backing of Don Juan for his claim to the regency, a claim possibly more suitable in view of all the enemies made by the old Infante Juan through the years. Don Juan Manuel, promised heaven and earth by the power-seeking young Pedro (Giménez Soler, pp. 413–14), agreed to give him his influential support. The wily Infante Juan first corralled the vote of Juan Núñez and then assembled the town councils of León, one of his main power bases, at Benavente to have them vote in his favor. At Coca the party of the other pretender brought together a junta of municipal councils, plus Juan Manuel and the Haro family, for the same purpose. Don Juan did not take a very vigorous role in this political campaigning, simply following his father-in-law's counsel to back his brother-in-law. Eventually both Infantes were declared regents (Giménez Soler, pp. 451–55), together with María de Molina, for Alfonso's minority. The two queens, Fernando's widow and his mother, were living in Toro, to which Don Juan Manuel made a visit with Pedro for the ceremony of recognition for the latter.

The years 1313–1314 saw Don Juan embroiled in difficulties on two accounts: At first there were signs that the mutual respect he and the regent Pedro had proclaimed was quickly deteriorating, and then there were much more serious aggravations between

Don Juan and his nominal subjects in Murcia. Don Juan was never a man to forget even the smallest detail of any agreement he considered honorably made; hence his great rage, contained at first, upon gradually becoming aware that Pedro did not intend to fulfill the promise, given in return for Don Juan's support, to provide him with the local powers of *tutor* in certain bishoprics in which Don Juan's holdings were extensive: Cuenca, Toledo, Sigüenza. At one point, Don Juan in disgust affiliated his name with the group (including the young king's mother, the Infanta Constanza of Portugal) opposed to the Cortes-recognized *tutores*, and when Pedro sought him out for continued discussions, Don Juan remained quietly in a fortified dwelling in Valdecañas belonging to a Guillén de Rocafull and refused to see him. Before being called away on another hurried trip to Murcia to see to defenses against Moslem incursions, Don Juan apparently decided to forget the past promises of regent-like powers in the mentioned episcopates, since he would now be satisfied to recover his former powers as comptroller (*mayordomo*) within the kingdom's bureaucracy relinquished when Pedro became regent. He also wished to be reimbursed with a large sum of money for his allegiance, money to be used to acquire lands in Castile currently in the name of the Portuguese Infanta. When it appeared that this conflict over promises between Don Juan and Pedro might be settled peacefully with the Archbishop of Toledo as arbiter, Don Juan suddenly seized an opportunity to show his rage by committing an act that could have led to serious reprisals, had it not been for the restraint displayed by others at the time. The head of the Order of Calatrava, a prominent figure who had originally made the promises personally on behalf of Pedro, was actually seized and held prisoner by Don Juan, who then boldly informed his father-in-law (Giménez Soler, p. 442) that the Maestre of Calatrava would not be released until the demands were satisfied. Jaime exploded with rage, first writing a blistering letter of accusation to Don Juan, and then asking Pedro to forget the shameful deed. Jaime also promised that the Maestre would be released forthwith and asked that Pedro proceed to reach an accord with Don Juan. An agreement (Giménez Soler, pp. 447–48) between the Infante and Don Juan was signed in May, 1314.

With this settled, however, Don Juan saw himself again deceived as Pedro moved quickly to purchase the very lands that

Don Juan sought to buy with the money now promised by Pedro. Don Juan vented his rage in customary fourteenth-century style by riding into his enemy's land and committing acts of destruction and theft. This matter too was apparently solved (amazingly enough, with the Maestre of Calatrava as arbiter) by splitting the villages between Don Juan (Alcocer) and Pedro (Cifuentes and Peñas de Viana). Don Juan was to pay indemnities for the destruction caused by his raids on royal lands.

II *Continuing Difficulties in Murcia; The Challenge of Rocafull*

One of the more unsavory episodes in Don Juan Manuel's political career now began to take shape in the correspondence of 1314–1315: the intense animosity shown by the Murcians and their Concejo toward their royally appointed administrator, Don Juan Manuel. It is difficult to adduce the specific reasons for their feelings of hate and fear. They were to take extraordinary measures, such as demanding assurances from the Aragonese king against revenge by Don Juan and even proclaiming a local *caudillo* (Giménez Soler, p. 456), one Berenguer de Puigmoltó, to support their cause. It is not difficult, however, to imagine why they would fear Don Juan's actions, for he could be extremely vindictive and demanding when involved in a struggle over something he considered rightfully his. At one point he threatened the Council with exclusion from his nonaggression treaty with Granada and thus would expose them to possible attacks. That such an act would not bring about affection for him among the Murcians did not occur to him, for in the fourteenth century force was what settled matters and Don Juan knew how to apply it. In the course of this continuing clash over the Adelantamiento of Murcia, in which Pedro was accused of complicity in the Murcian rebellion against Don Juan, the latter delivered a vicious raid against Pedro's possessions at Berlanga on the Duero, wishing to make clear to Pedro his intention to have his way. As usual in quarrels between the powerful, the little people paid the highest price.

On the heels of a second settlement, at Uclés in January, 1315, of the disagreements between Don Juan Manuel and the Infante Pedro, there occurred later that year an unusual incident about which we can only deduce the surface details. The underlying antagonisms of this unpleasant moment in Don Juan's life, never mentioned in his works, may never be fully known. Toward the middle of 1315, in the presence of none other than María de Molina and the other regents of the young king, a man of some wealth named Guillén de Rocafull challenged Don Juan Manuel to personal combat in the field. The correspondence (Giménez Soler, pp. 464–68) reveals that the formulaic name-calling ordinarily used in such *rieptos* was, in this case, strongly objected to by the Infante Juan, who wrote to Jaime II stating that the vicious language used by the Catalan Rocafull amounted to an action contemptible by Castilian standards. What Don Juan was called or exactly what level of language was used is not known, but primarily we do not and may never know what action of Don Juan brought on this challenge. Such challenges between titled *fijosdalgo* were perfectly legal in Castile, as may be seen in fourteenth-century regional and municipal laws. There appears to be little doubt about where Don Juan committed the act that produced the wrath of the Catalan: in Rocafull's own thick-walled and well-protected house in Valdecañas in Castile where the Catalan owned property, and where Don Juan had once been Rocafull's guest. Thus the incident must have been something personal and of an extraordinary nature, since word of it spread far and wide, and the two men were to hate each other as long as they lived. After the challenge had been hurled in Don Juan's face, the Infante Pedro caused Rocafull to be held forcibly, accusing him of an improper action. His release was brought about by the many voices who apparently spoke up against Don Juan. Thereafter, a number of attempts were made to hold a hearing with everyone present, but Don Juan steadfastly refused to participate. It was even proposed (Giménez Soler, p. 468) by one of the regents (Juan) that he (Juan Manuel) attend a hearing protected by a thousand men on horse.

III   *The Regents' Deaths on the Granada Plain*

This period following the solution of the problems of regency during Alfonso's minority was not one of peace. Indeed the constant turmoil caused by ambitious barons and magnates left the Castilian countryside in a continual state of distress, to which bands of roving thieves spreading terror added a further measure of the same. The internal tribulation is best depicted by the Aragonese envoy to Castile, whose appointed function was simply to give as clear a picture of the situation as possible. What is also clear from his reports (Giménez Soler, p. 466) is that the younger of the two regents, Pedro, encouraged by his mother, María de Molina (a woman herself of great prestige and highly respected by the people), was vigorously exercising his powers to improve conditions in Castile. The old Infante Juan aided with the day-to-day management of Castilian affairs at María's side, whenever the fiery and well-liked Pedro rode off to engage in battle on the Andalusian frontier. It must have been apparent to the Infante Juan that in any future disagreement with Pedro, the latter, with everyone's backing, would have his way.

Don Juan Manuel, thirty-four years old in 1316 and upset over the absence of a male heir, found to his sorrow that his wife Constanza's sickly condition had been diagnosed as tubercular (*ética* is the common fourteenth-century expression) by the Catalan physician of his father-in-law. The grieving Aragonese monarch pleaded with Don Juan to send her for a spell to Valencia, where she had been born and raised, and where he could provide an array of doctors and a greater variety of medicinal preparations. Don Juan, who never really trusted the physicians of others (a belief emphasized in the *Unfinished Book,* Chap.2), kept her in the care of his physicians in the colder climate of the meseta. Mention may be made here of a victorious encounter by Don Juan in 1317 with Moslems along the Murcian frontier near Lorca (Giménez Soler, pp. 471–72). This was an occasion in which a victory was achieved where a defeat had just been suffered.

One of the most startling events of the entire Reconquest was now (1318–1319) about to take place. It would lead eventually to a new junta of regents during Alfonso XI's minority, in which Don Juan Manuel would assume the ruling powers of a *tutor* for the crown of Castile. The backdrop to this extraordinary turn of affairs in Castile was formed by internal political instability in Nasrid Granada, where Nasir I had been deposed by the rebellious caudillo from Málaga, Sa'id Farach, who placed his son Abu 'l-Walid Isma'il in the Alhambra. A struggle for control of all Granada had followed between Isma'il and Nasir, the latter having been ordered away to rule Guadix to the east. In the early stages of this struggle in 1312, Fernando IV had collapsed and died as he approached with an army to aid the cause of Nasir. A letter written in Catalan in the Alhambra from Isma'il to Jaime II in 1314 indicates that Nasir by this time had been effectively forced to remain in Guadix. A lull in activity by the Christians ensued, but the energetic Pedro as regent was soon enticed by Nasir's promise (Giménez Soler, pp. 449–50) to turn over Guadix to Castile if he would aid him seize Granada. The Guadix kingdom was extensive, its border running through Baza and Vera (Almería), and hence bordering on the southern edge of Murcia. Don Juan Manuel, as Adelantado of Murcia, had maintained a truce along this frontier with Nasir, and even with Nasir's predecessor in Guadix, and therefore was not involved at this time in any concerted military action, apart from a raid or two, such as the one at Lorca. It is possible that these attacks were attempts by Don Juan to arouse sentiment for the Reconquest and to obtain a large share of the funds the Papacy donated for the Reconquest, which he wished to pursue on a grand scale; the expulsion of the Moor is a theme in his works. Yet his close personal friendship with Nasir might explain in part his objective portrayal of aspects of Moslem civilization in the fiction of the *Lucanor*; he relishes mentioning in *Estados* (II, 3) his conversations with learned Moslems who listen to reason. It has also been suggested that his vanity may have caused him to be envious of the exploits of the exuberant Pedro.

The two regents now planned a mighty aggression in 1319 against internally weak Granada, one that would provide a definitive solution. Cambil and the supposedly impregnable Tixcar had fallen to Pedro in preliminary raids, in one of which he rode to within a very few miles of Granada itself. A large Christian force under both regents then moved into the Vega, setting up camp before Granada on the eve of St. John, a Saturday. The *Chronicle of Alfonso XI* states (*BAE*, 66, pp. 181–84) that on Sunday the Infantes argued their next move, and the withdrawal suggested by Juan began on Monday, a day described in later accounts as one of intense heat. The rear guard under the older Infante was suddenly attacked by the cavalry of the Moroccan leader Abu Sa'id Uthman, and panic swept through most of the Christian force. Pedro had a seizure of some kind trying to rally his men to hold ranks and dropped dead from his horse. Hearing this news, the aged Juan had an apoplectic fit and was dead by nightfall. The advance units of the Christian army fled at word of Pedro's death. Don Juan Manuel, mentioning this disaster in *Estados* (I, 77), adds a remarkable eulogy to Moslem horsemen and their theory of war. He severely criticizes the Christian cavalry's tendency to let themselves be drawn into attacking in small, disorganized numbers, a game (*espolonadas a tornafuy*) the outnumbered Moor enticed the Christian to play. The slower, clumsier Christian, often loaded with booty, was soon ridden to his death.

IV *The Crisis of 1319–1325*

And once again beleaguered Castile was to face a crisis of leadership. With Pedro dead, another living son of Sancho IV was the Infante Felipe, who by character appeared generally unfit to lead. The minor Alfonso's grandmother, María de Molina, was still living; when she talked, everyone listened, but given her age, sixty, and less than adequate health, she could in no sense govern Castile. One man seemed a more logical choice than most for the regency: Don Juan Manuel.

Don Juan, following his repeated dictum that the wellborn must naturally try to increase their wealth and prestige, set about actively to obtain the regency. Jaime advised him (Giménez Soler, pp. 478–79) not to act rashly, but to think only of serving God and his King, and the matter would take care of itself. Don Juan rarely followed such a course. He obtained recognition as regent from several municipal councils in Cuenca and Albacete and other areas of eastern Extremadura in Castile where his influence was strong. ("Extremadura," in the fourteenth century, is anywhere along the southern edge of Christian territory in a half-moon strip curving from Badajoz and Huelva eastward.) Don Juan visited Valladolid to speak in his own behalf to the revered María. Unsuccessful there, he dared, quietly, to enter unfriendly cities, such as Salamanca (from which he had to flee on foot), in Old Castile and León, in a search for political adherents. Burgos meanwhile, still considered the heart, if not the head, of the kingdom, despite Valladolid, was the scene of an alliance of northern nobles under Don Juan el Tuerto (son of the Infante Juan; the epithet *Tuerto* refers to his misshapen body), who all swore to unite in recognizing a regent of their choice. María de Molina, the surviving *tutora*, refused to call the Cortes into session as long as tensions were unrelieved; an enormous amount of time was spent in recovering the Infantes' cadavers, a topic later to become a ballad favorite, for burial at Las Huelgas in Burgos.

In this impasse, Don Juan Manuel, María, and her son Felipe agreed in May, 1320, to exercise authority individually in those areas already committed to them and to cease quarreling among themselves. When the time was ripe, they would rule, according to tentative plans, the uncommitted regions jointly. The results of all this in realistic terms, however, were negative. Violent disagreements occurred within the triumvirate above, as well as with other landed families. These disputes over rights to dispense justice and collect taxes in this or that village were never settled satisfactorily; there was simply no machinery set up to accomplish that. To satisfy a claim of invasion of territorial rights, one raided the property of his enemy, burned buildings, stole cattle, razed crops.[1]

V   The Archbishop of Toledo

In May, 1320, a noteworthy ceremony took place in Toledo: the investiture of a new archbishop of that city, who would naturally also be, in name at least, Primate of "all the Spains"; in the present situation in Castile, he would likewise be *canciller*, i.e., first secretary and keeper of the kingdom's seal, a post of importance, but largely honorary (someone else was appointed *canciller mayor*) and ordinarily held in Castile by this prelate, much as León's *canciller* had been the archbishop of Santiago. What was noteworthy was none of the above, however, but the age of the new archbishop (he was just reaching his twentieth birthday) and his nationality (he was not Castilian but Aragonese, the third son of Jaime II, the Infante Juan). The appointment of archbishops lay ultimately with the Pope (in this case, John XXII), and Juan's age for this post, while youthful even by fourteenth-century standards, was not so young as might appear in the modern view. The Infante had early attained a reputation for his brilliant mind; tonsured by Clement V himself in Avignon, his solid classical training (he and his father generally corresponded in Latin) had been acquired at Scala Dei, the ascetic Carthusian house in Tarragona. An educated nineteen-year-old in the fourteenth century could function to a degree in his society that a nineteen-year-old today would find impossible. Juan's nationality, nevertheless, was another matter altogether. The fact that an Aragonese king, through an envoy in Rome and an agent in Toledo, a man named Diego García, had been successful in having his son named to this post brought on varying degrees of anxiety for political reasons throughout all Castile. The success of this planning was due primarily to one man, Diego García. Don Juan Manuel apparently thought that his own interests would in no way suffer and might even be improved by the presence of a brother-in-law in this high post in Toledo. Yet Don Juan could become quite resentful whenever he felt that a situation involving him was being contrived without his active help, and it is possible that he felt increased animosity toward Diego García, a man he had disagreed with in the past.[2]

The struggles over the rights of regency, meanwhile, punctuated with bursts of bloody violence, heightened considerably, to the great detriment, as usual, of the countryfolk. The municipal council of Talavera, in April, 1320, had agreed to recognize the right of Don Juan Manuel to exercise the powers of regent, and the latter in turn promised them financial relief in the upkeep of the ring of castles maintained for protection locally. Thus went the bargaining, amid a continuous round of broken and newly formed allegiances. Guadalajara, refusing to recognize Don Juan as *tutor* in its district, felt the force of his anger late in 1320, the bloodshed being reported to an Aragonese agent by a Moslem held prisoner in Guadalajara at the time (Giménez Soler, pp. 490–91). Segovia next fell into line as the bishop, deans, and canons of its cathedral and collegiate churches swore to support Don Juan as regent with the aged María, but with no mention of her son Felipe; Don Juan at once reaffirmed (Giménez Soler, pp. 491–92) this bishopric's privileges and rights. And so went the maneuvering in anticipation of the next session of the Cortes. It would soon be Toledo's turn to speak.

At this point, early in 1321, John XXII had become so distraught at the news from Castile that he was to send Cardinal de Santa Sabina to the peninsula to attempt to bring the opposing factions together. The Cardinal, traveling to Toledo and elsewhere, had begun conferences with Don Juan Manuel, the Queen Grandmother, and others. Then, ready to use his office and that of the Pope as a means of pressuring the parties into an agreement, he called for a Council to take place in Palencia even as María de Molina was calling for the Cortes to be assembled at Valladolid.

Still in the first year of his post in Toledo, the Archbishop was approached by Don Juan Manuel with the request that he be sanctioned officially and openly by the Archbishop as the only regent acceptable to himself and to Toledo. (The *reino de Toledo* occupied in the fourteenth century the bulk of what is now called New Castile.) When the young prelate refused, Don Juan reacted furiously, and a chain of events ensued that, in view of the situation, would probably end tragically, in one way or another.

VI *The Murder of Diego García*

A letter was sent from Alcalá in May, 1321, on orders of Abbot Raimundo of the royally protected Aragonese monastery of Monte Aragón (Huesca), who sought to inform the King of Aragon of the tense situation now developing between his son the Archbishop and Don Juan Manuel. This abbot and other authorities, civil and religious, including the Masters of Santiago and Calatrava, were meeting in vain attempts to achieve some measure of peace in the country. The abbot described the strong pressures and threats employed by Juan Manuel to force a public proclamation from the Archbishop. The Infante Juan stated his case plainly: His obedience was due only to the Pope who wished him to act as mediator for the common good. Don Juan threatened that Toledo would enjoy peace only if the Archbishop set his hand and seal to the announcement. When the latter refused, stating he must seek his father's counsel, there were again extremely harsh words from Juan Manuel, who then abruptly announced that the Archbishop was not a man whose word he could now accept.

Three days later, three days apparently spent in impotent rage waiting for the tide to run in his favor, Don Juan called Diego García to his presence in the alcázar, where he was seized, taken aside, and murdered. Diego García's wife and son, responding to a call from Don Juan to come to recover the body, were also suddenly seized and held. At this point the area of the alcázar became heavily fortified with Don Juan's men and the mood of the city was one of disorganization and fright. At noon the next day, Don Juan agreed to meet with representatives of a group of citizens who sought the return of Diego García. Don Juan explained that Diego García and an accomplice, Garcilaso (de la Vega), had planned to murder the young king, and a public display was needed, whereupon he at once ordered the corpse hurled into the street from the tower room where the murder had taken place. Don Juan will state his belief in a single example-setting act of violence to clear the air: *es muy grant mester de mostrar ante braveza et gran crueldat (Estados I, 69)*. His possessions confiscated, his family imprisoned, the body of Diego García would be buried without honor.

The Archbishop, in Diego García's debt for the latter's many services, was greatly shaken by the stark brutality of the incident. As a letter arrived from María de Molina, warmly urging him to take part in the Cortes, he wrote asking her forgiveness and saying that the weather was too hot. Don Juan Manuel held Toledo in a viselike grip.

The facts above have been taken largely from the Abbot's confidential narration of events (Giménez Soler, pp. 496–98) for his sovereign, and there being no imaginable reason why he, apparently either a witness or in receipt of firsthand information, would lie in a secret letter to the King of Aragon, we can safely assume that they represent the truth to the extent that any such narration can. It is difficult to believe that Diego García's political status was what mattered to Don Juan Manuel on the day of his vengeance, May 17, 1321. Even granting the great degree of political influence wielded by Diego García and its possible utilization, it is unlikely that at this point in the chain of events this was the primary or the sole reason for the murder. (One of the men charged by Don Juan, in the "official" reason for his actions, with planning the murder of the ten-year-old Alfonso, Garcilaso de la Vega, would be one of Alfonso's three closest associates at his majority in 1325.) Don Juan Manuel committed this atrocious act because (1) it was apparent that the Cortes would soon reach some accord on the regency, and he knew that he would not be given the lion's share he felt he merited, with or without the backing of Toledo; (2) he saw on all hands, especially after a scolding from Cardinal de Santa Sabina, a united and increasing opposition to his assuming a controlling share of the regency, and there was no doubt that before the Cortes the aged and dying María would speak with a voice louder than his; (3) he was at that moment more obsessed with political power than at any other moment in a lifetime spent in pursuit of such power; (4) his rage at the Archbishop's (his brother-in-law's) refusal was obviously such that he had reached the point of not being able to think of anything else; and, most importantly, (5) he sought to display before his fellowmen his state of mind at that moment in the most destructive manner possible, namely, murdering, in outrageously public fashion, a prominent individual who was an intimate adviser and close friend of the Archbishop, and who also happened to be a man who had opposed him in the past.

Don Juan Manuel did not expect to gain Toledo's vote by this act. What he wished to do, and what he did, was spread fear, brutally hold the city under iron-like military control, and effectively create a situation in which Toledo had little or no voice in matters before the assembled Cortes. Don Juan wanted all Castile, and especially Toledo, over which he claimed to be master, to know how he felt at that moment, as well as to satisfy himself vengefully against the prelate. The latter was considered a relative acting treacherously by not acceding to Don Juan's wishes, and in his works Don Juan finds few men so low as the individual who only poses as a friend while making promises: *ca muy grant vergüença es fazer el señor bien a un omne et desfazerlo después* (*Estados* I, 69). The bloody strife among the pretenders to power would become even bloodier after the death in June that same year of María de Molina, and the absence of what prudence and wisdom she brought to bear.

VII   A New Regency and the Accession of Alfonso XI to the Throne

The Cortes called into assembly in April did little to assuage the uneasy situation. Shortly before her death, María de Molina had wisely insisted that the municipal council of Valladolid retain all authority in overseeing the care and upbringing of the youthful heir to the crown; she clearly knew what she was doing, even on her deathbed. Another tripartite *tutoría* (Don Juan Manuel, Don Juan el Tuerto, the Infante Felipe) was elected, and for the next five years, until Alfonso XI was prematurely declared of age, the country remained in a state of internal chaos; attempts on Don Juan Manuel's life are described in *Estados* I,

62. Don Juan and the Archbishop, encouraged by Jaime II to respect each other, did not have to make a great effort in that direction immediately, since the prelate left Castile for an ostensibly short visit to Valencia to be with his family. He remained in Aragon for a year. After his return, he was to have a violent exchange of words with Don Juan Manuel (in 1324) over the latter's heavy taxes imposed in Toledo, causing the Aragonese monarch to rebuke Don Juan strongly. The reader of this correspondence may wish to reserve some sympathy for Constanza, caught in the struggle between husband and brother; her letters to her father try with some difficulty to relate the developing antagonisms.

After a reconciliation in 1325, surely influenced in part by Constanza's deteriorating health, Don Juan would begin two of his works with epistles to his brother-in-law, asking him to excuse the defects in his literary endeavors and to appreciate his good intentions. The Infante Juan was a man with literary interests himself. He and his sister Constanza were always the closest of friends, perhaps drawn together as "exiles" in a dangerously disorganized Castile; and the Infante was held in the greatest esteem in his homeland, if his extraordinary tomb in the Tarragona cathedral is any indication. An inquiry might be made into the many possible reasons Don Juan chose to address these works to the Infante, but it is unlikely that any startling conclusions would be reached. Don Juan is now entering that period of his life in which he is turning with increased interest to the composition of his works.

In interviews in 1324 between Bernardo de Sarriá, the brilliant counsel for the Crown of Aragon, and Don Juan Manuel, the latter persisted, as he had for some time, in trying to arrange a marriage between Alfonso XI and a daughter of the King of Aragon. His interests were purely those of self-aggrandizement: A marriage that would enhance his political posture in the future. In view of the recent bitter exchanges between Don Juan and Jaime, there must have been a patently false note about Don Juan's present show of concern for Aragonese interests. Don Juan saw fit to warn Jaime that Alfonso XI, once in power, would disavow the treaties of 1304–1305 and move on Murcia; if it came to war against Aragon, Don Juan promised that he would fight at Jaime's side and be willing to lose everything he owned in

Castile. Jaime was no fool. He signed a sharp retort, prepared by the astute Sarriá, to these misrepresentations that was remarkably direct and dripping with sarcasm: ". . . we in Aragon know as well as you the identity of those who advise the King of Castile to go to war. And we know that they do this so that he is swayed from calling them to account for their wretched actions during his minority. But you are certainly not in their ranks since what greater honor could there be for you than that of having a sister-in-law on the throne of Castile [. . .] I would prefer to live in peace, but should that be impossible, we will certainly point out to our enemy the dreadful advice he has received from his advisers" (Giménez Soler, p. 508).

Late in the summer of 1325, the regents were ordered to Valladolid for the public ceremony of releasing their rights and accepting the new sovereign (Giménez Soler, pp. 512–13). Don Juan turned over the seal he had had cast and had used liberally for four years. Although the Cortes restored him to unreservedly full power in Murcia and granted him other favors, there are the beginnings of a suspicion that the new ring of advisers at the fourteen-year-old monarch's shoulder look with considerable disfavor on Don Juan Manuel and his close ally, Juan el Tuerto, the son of his old friend and hunting companion.

VIII   *The Betrothal of Constanza Manuel*

Accounts of the heartbreaking episode that now embitters the entire adult life of Constanza, daughter of Don Juan Manuel and his second wife, Constanza of Aragon, tend to stress that this sombre chapter occurs because of Don Juan's overweening pride and failure to foresee an obvious deception. Such accounts emphasize unduly certain aspects of the affair. What happened was this: Alfonso XI's advisers had looked with mistrust upon the alliance of Don Juan Manuel and Juan el Tuerto, two powerful barons with immense holdings in Old and New Castile, León, Vizcaya, and Murcia. These two, according to reports, had agreed to a pact of mutual aid. They had also determined that Constanza Manuel would marry el Tuerto and had solemnized their oaths at a mass in Cigales near Valladolid at which they received the Eucharist from the same host. With unusual celerity, advisers of the boy-king then appeared before Juan Manuel to suggest a marriage between Constanza and Alfonso, Don Juan accepted, and the Infante Felipe arrived in Peñafiel to take the betrothed child away to royal protection. Don Juan received strong property guarantees to back up the royal word and Giménez Soler has published letters (p. 531) from Constanza in which she refers to herself as *Reyna de Castiella et de Leon*. The Valladolid Cortes voted their approval of the marriage on November 28, 1325.

The first effect of this sudden appearance of bonds uniting the Alfonsine and Manueline houses was to loosen the formerly close ties between the latter and Juan el Tuerto. Although it will not be evident for some time, the idea of breaking up this coalition played no small part in inspiring the plan of Alfonso's advisors to propose a marriage that would never be finally blessed. At this point in 1326, Don Juan Manuel must have believed that he was the most powerful man in Castile; he certainly had reason to think so. And at this point he took a political step that was unfortunate indeed: Overwhelmed by a sense of his new political stature in Castile, he turned on the Aragonese royal family, urging that the Aragonese be thrown out of Murcia-Alicante. This was undoubtedly what Alfonso's advisers had been waiting to hear, since it had been their goal to weaken this coalition as well.

Yet it becomes easy to see why Don Juan accepted the bait so eagerly, if one only realizes how tempting the bait really was. It would have been so to most men, but to Don Manuel it must have been absolutely irresistible: his daughter on the throne of Castile, and her husband a fifteen-year-old. If he had any doubts, they disappeared when he considered what he thought to be the true situation: The youthful monarch, unsteady in those first months of his reign, needed the support of Don Juan Manuel. This is exactly the sentiment that appears in Don Juan's correspondence at this time. Little did he suspect the violent nature, latent, but soon active, in the fifteen-year-old. The boy Alfonso, as it turned out, bore no psychological resemblance to his father, the inept Fernando, but was his grandfather, Sancho the Fierce, reborn.

It was not long before Alfonso's intentions were suspect. A brief delay was necessary to send someone to Rome to obtain the dispensation needed since the betrothed were related, even though only very remotely, with Jaime I the Conqueror the link (the latter's daughter had married Alfonso X). This presented no real problem, yet the courier had to pass through Aragon, and Don Juan was apparently too embarrassed to seek safe-conduct directly from his father-in-law; Don Juan's wife had to write to her brother, asking for letters of recommendation. Somehow matters began to drag. The courier, the chapter head of the Cuenca cathedral, returned empty-handed. Don Juan swallowed his pride, went to the Archbishop of Toledo, and asked him to intercede with Rome. The Archbishop kindly agreed. Now growing uneasy, Don Juan went off to Granada in July, 1326, meeting and defeating Uthman in a clash on the Guadalhorce River (Málaga).

Then, with what must have been cold foreboding, Don Juan received some news from Castile: Don Juan el Tuerto, who had been riding destructively through royal lands, was induced, after receiving guarantees of his safety, to go to Toro to meet Alfonso, who had him and his two aides killed on the spot. Profoundly shaken by this incident, Don Juan proceeded north to Cuenca, secluding himself in the castle at Garcimuñoz. He sent letters to Jaime II warning that the honor of both was endangered. Now frightened, he sought out his Aragonese relatives, even the Archbishop, asking their assistance as he feared the worst. Don Juan remained in his castles, out of touch with Castilian political circles, and as Alfonso now talked of marrying a Portuguese Infanta, the deception became unmistakably clear. His honor tested, Don Juan began equipping large numbers of armed men, and a period of mutual distrust began that would end in armed conflict at Escalona and Huete between the King and Don Juan. In his works the latter will lament how impossible it is to avoid war once preparations have begun.

Don Juan publicly declared himself not a subject of the King of Castile, as what was in reality imprisonment in the castle at Toro, cruel and inexcusable, began for Constanza; Alfonso XI refused to have her released. Just as her mother of the same name had spent many early years as a child protected in the castle of Villena and awaiting a marriage at twelve to Juan Manuel (then thirty), Constanza now too would suffer in Toro, for no real reason other than the malevolence of the men in her life. The rejected, disillusioned child, a pawn used disgracefully in these political games, will find herself again betrothed a decade later to Pedro, heir to the crown of Portugal.[3] The ill will of the Portuguese king was now added to that of the rest, since his idea in proposing the marriage of Constanza and his son was to join Don Juan and find satisfaction for an affront to his daughter, the wife of Alfonso XI. The latter had soon abandoned his new Portuguese wife, the Queen, and was in the process of having his famous affair with the Sevillian beauty Leonor de Guzmán, an affair that never ended and produced five bastard sons, the eldest of whom would begin the Trastámara dynasty in Castile in 1369 after putting a knife into the body of his half-brother, the King, after the battle of Montiel.

Alfonso found it relatively easy to prevent the celebration of the Pedro-Constanza marriage (already a fact on paper, but not to be consummated until years later), by denying Constanza, who had taken refuge from Alfonso XI in Aragon, permission to cross his lands into Portugal. (For this and other reasons, Don Juan would later again publicly reject his loyalty to the monarch.) At long last, permission was obtained, as part of the Portuguese-Castilian treaty of Seville in 1340, for Constanza to join Pedro in Portugal and consummate a marriage that had been legal since Pedro's fifteenth birthday in 1336. Her husband, as if fate had already decided against her all along, was the Infante Pedro who would fall in love with his wife's lady-in-waiting, Inés de Castro, a comely Galician girl. His legendary moment of madness in exhuming his dead mistress for a cadaverous coronation, after he became king, would enliven peninsular drama for years to come.[4]

IX *The Death of Constanza of Aragon*

The tragic history of his daughter Constanza may have been the most humiliating and frustrating episode in Don Juan Manuel's life. The death of her mother occurred in September, 1327; and the death two months later of Jaime II profoundly weakened Don Juan's ties with Aragon and the support he often counted on in the past. Don Juan's second wife, Constanza of Aragon, died after a long struggle with her tubercular condition; her letters to her father often pointedly mentioned her physical condition, and Don Juan had asked her father earlier in 1327 to send Catalan physicians to care for her.[5] She apparently had suffered a nervous breakdown early in 1327, upset at seeing her daughter imprisoned in Toro, for Don Juan spoke of her desire to enter a convent and of her being strangely sad and depressed: *fío por la su merçed que muy ayna será fuera de todas aquellas ymaginaçiones que solía aver.*

Life seemed especially cruel to Constanza of Aragon. The two sons she bore Don Juan Manuel died as children; after the death of the first, her father had advised her (Giménez Soler, p. 501) not to raise the second one with the advice of the family Jewish physicians whom Don Juan always trusted implicitly. She had a second daughter by Don Juan, Beatriz, who, like Constanza, lived to adulthood. At this point (1327), Don Juan Manuel was forty-five years old and without a male heir, a circumstance he found most distressing.

X *War with Alfonso XI; Marriage to Blanca Núñez*

In Zafra (Cuenca, not Badajoz) in December, 1327, in the midst of his first open rebellion, Don Juan Manuel composed an extraordinary series of communications to his subordinates in Murcia calling for attacks on the crown (Giménez Soler, pp. 551–58). These letters, as well as other signed cartes blanches for the Moslem King of Granada, promising him *castiellos e villas* (castles and towns) for his aid against Alfonso and asking him for two thousand horsemen to *estragar Castiella fata dallende de Toledo* (lay waste to the land even north of Toledo [!]) were all intercepted almost immediately by the very man (Pero López de Ayala) Alfonso had appointed as Adelantado of Murcia after removing Don Juan from that position. In January, 1328, the couriers, all close associates of Don Juan Manuel, were dismembered on orders of Alfonso, their eyes cut out, and their throats cut. Skirmishes and an occasional siege took place that spring; Don Juan surrounded Huete in March, cutting off its water and setting up *engennos,* devices for the destruction and scaling of walls. No clear-cut decision would be reached in this conflict of lord and vassal, despite Don Juan's avowed intention to *faser la mas crua guerra* (carry out as much destruction as possible). It should be remembered, as his works are taken up, that Don Juan is ready at this point to die if necessary for the sake of his honor; with his daughter and his name so vilified, it is difficult to argue that his rebellion was entirely without just cause.

Don Juan's close friend, Jaime de Jérica, a wealthy lord with lands in the Valencia-Alicante area adjacent to those of Don Juan in Alicante and Murcia, came to Peñafiel to fight at his side after seeking the approval (granted with misgivings) of his sovereign, Alfonso IV, the new King of Aragon. Against the lands of Don Juan in the southeast of the peninsula, rode, on orders of Alfonso XI, his former aide, Pero López de Ayala, and Guillén de Rocafull; the latter, thirteen years earlier, had insulted Don Juan in the royal presence in an attempt to establish grounds for a trial by combat. Rocafull was urged by the Castilian monarch (Giménez Soler, pp. 564–65) to avenge his earlier losses and persecution at the hands of Don Juan. Alfonso XI was also successful in driving his rebellious vassal further from his former Aragonese friends as his sister Leonor became the bride of Alfonso IV and Queen of Aragon. This amazingly is the same Leonor who had been married to Jaime II's first son nine years earlier in a nuptial mass at Gandesa and was abandoned literally on the church steps by the heir to the crown of Aragon, who determined he would rather wear the habit of a Hospitaller.[6] The weak Alfonso IV, for the rest of his brief indecisive reign (to 1336), would be inclined to do whatever his Castilian queen suggested; Alfonso could no longer be counted on by his former brother-in-law, Don Juan Manuel.

The struggle wore on intermittently into 1329. Pope John again sent emissaries to encourage both sides to make peace and join in a war against Granada, a frontier action Alfonso XI now eagerly anticipated but could not undertake with an enemy in his house. And now that enemy was suddenly stronger, for Don Juan Manuel had taken another wife, his third, Blanca Núñez of the line of Cerda, granddaughter of Fernando de la Cerda, Alfonso el Sabio's first-born. With this marriage to a wealthy bride, Don Juan could replenish his rapidly vanishing treasury, used up in hiring and equipping a small army; he would complain later that his struggles with Alfonso left him without any financial resources (*mucho afincado de mengua de dineros*). In October, 1329, the Bishop of Oviedo arranged a pact between the King and Don Juan that called for the latter to remain active on the Murcian front whenever Alfonso was attacking Granada (Giménez Soler, p. 578). To keep Don Juan off his back Alfonso agreed to restore him to his post as Adelantado of Murcia; to increase his authority on the southern front (this is the title referred to in the *Unfinished Book* [*prologue*]: *adelantado mayor de la frontera et del Bega*); to release Constanza Manuel from the castle at Toro; and to cancel indemnities for damage done by Don Juan to royal lands. The reappointment to the posts in Andalusia was greatly prized by Don Juan. It did not sit well with the Murcians, however, who still detested their former governor and had shown their displeasure with Don Juan's rule during his revolt against Alfonso by accusing him of treating his subjects harshly and dispossessing and exiling many prominent citizens. Their basic claim seemed generally to be that Alfonso X had declared them to be subjects only of the King. Alfonso XI promised them that he would correct past wrongs and prevent any abuses of power, and Don Juan early in 1330 again assumed his former powers in Murcia. He nevertheless avoided sessions of Cortes and the company of Alfonso for a long period, evidently spending his time hunting and reading and writing. He would claim later (*Estados* I, 70) that he had made enormous sacrifices and had done everything humanly possible to keep his honor intact. He still felt deeply a streak of bitterness toward Alfonso.

XI *Continuing Troubles with the Crown*

A period of barely controlled hostility between Don Juan Manuel and the Castilian King now begins, which will last in greater or lesser degree until the former's death in 1348. It is true that in the historic battles on the Salado River in 1340 and at Algeciras in 1343–1344 Don Juan will participate at the monarch's side, but these are interludes that may be misconstrued. In 1343, in any case, Don Juan will be sixty-one years old, a very old man for the fourteenth century; Juan Ruiz is believed by some (probably inaccurately) to be sitting unhappily in prison that year touching up the second version of his *Book of Good Love*; Pero López de Ayala, the stern satirist of the late fourteenth-century scene, is a boy ten years old.

Don Juan's long periods of absence from court affairs and withdrawal from political intrigue provided him with time to devote to the literary activities in which he was taking a greatly increased interest. If his friends scolded him for not joining them in the floating crap games of the era, he told them that he would rather spend his time with his books (*Unfinished Book*, 26).

Throughout the 1330's, Alfonso XI planned constantly to renew the Reconquest and destroy the Kingdom of Granada, plans that would culminate in the decisive victory on the Salado. Don Juan, however, showed little interest in the early thrusts of Castilian forces southward. His time was spent in Cuenca and Murcia, and the correspondence reveals that he more than once asked the Aragonese monarch to intercede with Alfonso on his behalf that he might act in conjunction with the Aragonese through Murcia rather than join forces with the King of Castile. These requests were granted. The attacks on the Murcian front nevertheless were extremely limited probings that razed a few fields and showed few real results. It is doubtful that they could have been more than that, in fact, since the rough, foreboding terrain between Cartagena and Almería offered little worth fighting for, and in no way could support a sizable army in the field for very long.

The Castilians meanwhile attacked by way of Jaén, complaining of the little accomplished by Don Juan and the Aragonese on the eastern front; Granada sought a treaty early in 1331, bringing to a close this series of thrusts by Alfonso. Don Juan had accompanied a week-long expedition of three thousand men out of Lorca for the purpose of raiding the lands around Vera and Huércal (Almería). It accomplished little of note, since there was probably very little that could be accomplished in that area. Breaking into the Moslem castles in the area was simply out of the question; they had no means of even remotely accomplishing that. The Murcia-Alicante region, therefore, was to remain relatively quiet during the thirties and forties. The *Chronicle of Alfonso XI* seeks to praise the Castilian King's efforts at reconquest by demeaning those of Don Juan. It is true that the latter's actions in this respect were insignificant; it is also true that his daughter had been disgraced, for which amends were not made, and that a deep sense of mistrust still separated the two men.

Alfonso XI had met Leonor de Guzmán (a relative of Alonso Pérez de Guzmán "el Bueno") before he became twenty. His rejection of his Portuguese wife, as he fell madly and permanently in love with the older Leonor, may have provided Don Juan with an idea for revenge against Alfonso. Giménez Soler believed that Don Juan suggested to Leonor that she encourage the young King to abandon his wife and make her the legitimate queen.

This was done purportedly to force Portugal to declare war on Castile. If this were the case, Leonor rejected the idea of becoming queen, and nothing came of it.

There is no doubt whatever that Don Juan did strive diligently on occasion to present an organized and hostile front against the King that would include himself, the Portuguese, the Nasrid Kingdom of Granada, and his new wife's brother, Juan Núñez. The latter, in a marriage planned by Don Juan Manuel, had taken as his wife María, the daughter of the murdered Juan el Tuerto, who had been living destitute in Bayonne; Núñez was eager now to recoup by war his dead father-in-law's property seized by Alfonso after the assassination in Toro. With such friends at home in Castile, Alfonso did not have to go look for enemies in the south.

At this juncture in the early 1330's, with agreements established between Alfonso XI's enemies and the King of Granada, the latter was able to reach further accords with the Merinid family ruling Morocco, and the son of the Moroccan Sultan, Abd al-Malik, now crossed the straits with an expeditionary force and laid siege to Gibraltar. The ominous shadow of Moroccan strength in Andalusia would grow, providing Alfonso with that much more reason to drive against the Moslem forces. Unlike his father, this Castilian King always seemed aware of the plots and counterplots around him. He knew that he could not proceed to Extremadura with wolves at the back door awaiting his departure; they either had to be fed or killed. At one point the latter solution was proposed by Alfonso for Don Juan Manuel, who was told by a member of the Haro family that the Castilian King had explicitly ordered his death. Finding the tense situation to his liking, Don Juan's brother-in-law, Juan Núñez, began terrifying towns in the royal domain. It was plain that Alfonso, with five thousand Moslem cavalry at Gibraltar's walls, had to make some decisive move without delay.

His first step was to send his falconer, a man already well known to Juan Manuel because of his profession, with an offer for the baron of Peñafiel: If the two Juans rode with him to Gibraltar, he would satisfy their demands for past aggrievances. This message was followed by an unusual series of meetings among the principals, the first of which were suggested by Juan Manuel. The extraordinary nature of these talks in Villaumbrales

(Valladolid) and Peñafiel in 1333 illuminates the then current relations between the King and his reluctant vassals.[7] Don Juan Manuel saw fit to kneel before his sovereign, ask forgiveness for wrongs committed, and pledge obedience and loyalty in the future. This gesture of good faith occurred on the road to Villaumbrales and must have been observed with curiosity by the aides in both parties. Before these good intentions could bear fruit, however, someone for some reason informed the two Juans that the one named Núñez would be murdered, that being one of the aims of Alfonso in these conferences. Juan Núñez then, although arriving at the next meeting armed and with an escort of soldiers, would not approach Alfonso. Don Juan Manuel told his monarch that he was ill and could not eat the food that Alfonso had ordered prepared for them that day. Word was sent on the following day suspending the talks; off to well-fortified Lerma went the master of Lara as the other Juan secluded himself in Peñafiel.

The tense situation went unrelieved as Alfonso, with Gibraltar on the verge of collapse, had to take action. He gave orders to all available forces to prepare to help raise the siege by the Moroccan forces, ignoring for the moment the two recalcitrant nobles who had already received royal funds to pay and outfit their troops, but who now demanded more funds for this purpose. Then, in one of those abrupt, unexpected maneuvers that Alfonso was given to taking on the spur of the moment, a trait which all along would inspire fear in the lords of Peñafiel and Lerma, the Castilian King twice made astonishing visits to Peñafiel itself, dining and chatting with Don Juan Manuel, and leaving the safety of his person entirely in his vassal's hands. On one of these secluded occasions, they discussed the threat to Castile's southern flanks so late into the evening that Don Juan's people thought that their master may have come to some harm. In these attempts to win over the confidence of Juan Manuel, and through the latter, to make an ally of Núñez, no signs of immediate success were visible. What can be said with certainty is that during June of that summer (1333) Alfonso reached Sevilla and his relief forces made a futile trip to Gibraltar, which had already fallen to the Moroccan and Granadan armies. Don Juan Manuel and Juan Núñez had offered to attack Granada via Jaén as their contribution to the effort, but neither carried through with these promises. Alfonso now signed a four-year truce with Granada (Giménez Soler, pp. 614–15) and, in a rage after almost a year's useless stay in Andalusia, headed north to take out his anger on the lords of Lerma and Peñafiel who, despite their actions, or the lack of them, could in no way have prevented the loss of Gibraltar.

Don Juan Manuel had real reason to worry now. An aroused Alfonso could be a fearfully vindictive man. Don Juan sought out the King of Aragon and, while proposing a marriage between his rejected Constanza and Alfonso IV's son, asked him to help resolve his differences with the King of Castile. During these talks the Aragonese monarch officially proclaimed Don Juan Manuel "Prince of Villena," an episode to flatter Don Juan's pride in his name and family line (Giménez Soler, p. 598). Aragon could do no more than this for him and would certainly have been unwilling to do more: the Queen of Aragon was Alfonso XI's sister.

The King of Castile meanwhile had reached Ciudad Real and his state of mind would soon become apparent to all. In this town the Bishop of Burgos made a presentation on behalf of the Aragonese royal family that described the intentions of Don Juan Manuel as honorable and invited Alfonso to visit his sister Leonor, so that an agreement of sorts might be worked out. Alfonso said that he could not visit his sister, since Juan Núñez must be dealt with, whereupon he ordered the mutilation of the next emissary, a man sent by Juan Núñez who wished to declare Núñez no longer a subject of the King of Castile. The man's feet, hands, and head were cut off; Alfonso had previously ordered a similar atrocity committed on Juan Manuel's messengers to the King of Granada in 1328, about which Don Juan complained bitterly in his rejection of loyalty to the crown. While this was taking place, the third body of messengers, sent by Juan Manuel and waiting to provide reasons for his absence from Andalusia, fled Ciudad Real in terror.

Most medieval sovereigns traveled constantly and covered great stretches of territory in their lifetimes, and the same was true of the noble class; few, however, would appear to move with the dispatch and decisiveness of Alfonso XI. Attempting to cut off the flight of Juan Núñez to Lerma in the spring of 1334, he completed the journey from Ciudad Real with great speed; in vain, as it turned out, since Núñez had been forewarned by paid informers. Deciding against a siege on heavily fortified and well-prepared Lerma, which would have taken an unforeseeable number of months, Alfonso drove eastward into La Rioja and the Basque lands to inflict damage on the third Juan among the trio of rebellious barons, this one a member of the Haro line, called in the chronicles "de los Cameros." This stay in the north brought on another period of tentative reconciliation among the major figures at cross-purposes that lasted through 1335. It was at this time that plans were laid, secretly at first, between Don Juan Manuel and the Portuguese King to marry Constanza Manuel to the Portuguese heir Pedro. The Castilian Infanta Blanca to whom Pedro had been married on paper apparently had contracted poliomyelitis and her paralytic condition, as attested by Castilian and Aragonese authorities examining the child at Portugal's request, provided sufficient grounds for annulment. There was still the problem of forcing Alfonso XI to allow Constanza to go to Portugal, since the Castilian King could seldom be forced to do anything.

Once more, then, Don Juan Manuel sought to oppose Alfonso XI with a united front of his forces and those of Lara and Haro plus the Portuguese, except that now, in January, 1336, with the death of Alfonso IV of Aragon, he hoped to encourage the new King of Aragon, the haughty Pedro IV, to join him as an ally. To this end his friend, the Peñafiel Prior Remón Masquefa, was successful in discussions with the new monarch. Thus armed with a treaty with Pedro IV "the Ceremonious," before which his recently acquired title was changed, doubtless at his own suggestion, from Prince to Duke of Villena, and in which he was supposed to swear he would cease minting coin in his castles, Don Juan Manuel publicly announced in July, 1336, that he was no longer a subject of Castile and owed no homage to its King (Giménez Soler, pp. 622–24). His reasons were several: Alfonso XI would not allow his daughter to proceed to Portugal for her marriage; the Castilian King sought to leave inheritances to the bastards he was proliferating with Leonor de Guzmán at the expense of other rightful heirs (especially those heirs of the property of Juan el Tuerto); the Castilian King was living in sin, failing to respect the honor and well-being of his legitimate wife and son; and Alfonso was likewise refusing a reasonable request to permit the Portuguese monarch to mediate these differences. This disavowal of allegiance to his King was sent to the King of Aragon to be recorded in that chancellery and other copies went to important public figures in Castile. No document was sent to Alfonso XI himself since, as Don Juan protested vehemently, he could find no one willing to deliver it; Alfonso was now well known for dismembering bearers of unpleasant news.

The real political situation in the peninsula remained nevertheless unchanged. The truth was simply that Alfonso XI moved too quickly and was too strong and decisive for any loose conglomerate of allies to force him into anything. The Portuguese took Badajoz, which they promptly abandoned upon hearing that Castilian *peones* (infantry) were marching in that direction (*Chronicle of Alfonso XI*, Chaps. 166–68). Juan Núñez, receiving the brunt of Alfonso's wrath, hid himself in Lerma, not daring to leave, as did Juan Manuel in Peñafiel, after successfully evading the soldiers sent to bring him to judgment (*Chronicle of Alfonso XI*, Chap. 163). To Don Juan's amazement, there in the town below could be seen one day the King himself, a sight to shake any man's nerve, and after that Don Juan quietly slipped away from Castile to Valencia.

Through the intercession of his mother-in-law Juana, Don Juan found himself again in the apparent good graces of Alfonso. This energetic female of Núñez de Lara stock had brought about a truce between her son and the King (Giménez Soler, p. 631; *Chronicle of Alfonso XI*, Chaps. 175–77), and then, with Don Juan Manuel's offer to turn over political control of Escalona to royal hands and level a number of his castles, she conferred with Alfonso and arranged an agreement of mutual trust signed by Don Juan in April, 1337, in Madrid. From this point through the Christian victories in 1340 and 1344, the relations of Don Juan with his sovereign were, on the surface at least, subdued and without calamitous procedures. A great part of this period found Don Juan in the company of Alfonso and his curia of associates, which is apparently where the King wished him to be, perhaps thinking this the safest arrangement to be contrived. At Cuenca Don Juan had performed that typically Castilian form of medieval homage, the kissing of the King's hands (*Estados* I, 86), and later was to serve as a spokesman for the King's sister

Leonor in Daroca in the mediation over her dispute with her stepson Pedro, who had been King of Aragon since her husband's death in 1336. Constanza Manuel was now permitted to join her husband in Portugal. Accompanying the king's coterie, especially that of this King, was not a way of maintaining an individual stance vis-á-vis the crown. Indeed it was a situation in which one can imagine only with some effort the strong and self-determining temperament of a loner like Don Juan Manuel.

Yet Alfonso must have known that such a procedure was necessary in the case of Don Juan, for the latter did not cease, despite this new relationship, maintaining with the King of Aragon secretive correspondence related to current matters discussed in Castile. The Prior of the Dominican house at Calatayud, Remón Guillén, served as intermediary in this continuing, apparently hidden alliance. In view of the threatening African forces being assembled in the south, however, the Kings of Aragon and Castile could only look in that direction for the time being.

XII   *Salado (1340) and Algeciras (1344); Death of Don Juan Manuel*

The Salado River is a trickle of water through the marsh-dotted land west of Tarifa (Cádiz). Near its banks on All Saints Eve in October, 1340, Alfonso XI led a massed force of primarily Castilian plus some Portugese troops against the combined Moroccan and Granadan armies of Abu-l-Hasan, Merinid Sultan of Fez, and Abu 'l-Hadjdjadj Yusuf I, King of Granada. In this massive encounter, in which the use of cannon, brought by the African forces from Damascus, was recorded for the first time in a battle in Europe, the annihilation of Moslem strength that ensued constitutes a major episode in the military history of the Reconquest. Any dream in Africa or Granada of ever recovering any part of the Moor's beloved al-Andalus now held by Christians was ended forever. The iron-like control of Alfonso XI over his men sent them three years later encircling Algeciras, where fought Chaucer's knight, in a long harsh siege that saw this premier Moslem port of entry capitulate in another bloody encounter. The loss of Algeciras cut the major Moslem supply route from Africa to Granada. Before Gilbraltar on Good Friday, 1350, death from the plague would overtake Alfonso XI at the age of thirty-nine. Had he lived a few more years, he would eventually have threatened and probably taken Granada itself, at that point prostrate and drained of men and goods. At least so thought the Moslem who wrote that Allah, in the passing of Alfonso at that time, saw fit to be merciful to his people. The last twenty years of Juan Manuel's life often appear to constitute one miscalculation after another in gauging the temperament of this king, whose violent responses to the situations facing him make him the strongest monarch in Castile, despite his impulsive character, in the fourteenth and fifteenth centuries.

In what seems a blatant effort to besmirch the name of Don Juan Manuel, the *Chronicle of Alfonso XI* (Chap. 251) injects an instance of cowardice on his part into its narration of the first of the two conflicts mentioned above. Whether the relating of this incident constitutes pure slander or whether, in fact, there is a basis of truth in it, and to what degree, are questions that remain unanswered. According to the chronicler, Don Juan, commanding the advance unit, refused under orders to send his troops across the Salado at the appointed time. As an added cutting touch, it is stated that he was taunted by an aide, the famous Jofre Tenorio, who noted that Don Juan's sword Lobera, his prized legacy from San Fernando that according to tradition no enemy could withstand, was not living up to expectations on that occasion; and that when Don Juan's first lieutenant overheard an urgent message from Alfonso XI to begin the crossing and moved forward with the flag, Don Juan struck the mounted officer a tremendous bash with his mace, knocking him to the ground. In sibylline tones the *Chronicle* warns that many present, seeing this, feared that Don Juan did not intend to serve his lord faithfully in this great undertaking. Over the years too much has been made over this possible incident in the life of the then fifty-eight-year-old Don Juan. One can take this passage as he wishes; he may regard it as something to be expected in a work often biased against Don Juan; he may choose to recall the long-standing animosity of Don Juan toward the King and, with this in mind, believe that it is entirely possible that Don Juan's actions were flawed to a degree on that All Saints Eve, and that Don Juan at the moment of truth could not see himself rushing head-long to his death for the greater glory in history of a man he privately detested.

In the *Poem of Alfonso XI* the verses on the Salado conflict refer to no such incident, but rather speak with praise of Don Juan's request to lead the advance unit and strike the first blow as a way of making amends for past sins against his fellowmen.[8] The *Poem* and the *Chronicle*, two works related in some undefined manner, are by different authors, with the poem believed to antedate the prose work. Both provide a substantial amount of detailed information about the battle on the Salado.

There is ample evidence that in other military campaigns in the early 1340's, both with Alfonso XI and as commander in his absence, Don Juan carried out his duties in responsible fashion. At the brutal siege of Algeciras Don Juan helped to repulse a Moslem breakout attempt that attacked his camp outside the walls. (The station adjacent to his was commanded by a boy who will become Pedro I of Castile.) Even here the *Chronicle* has its way of undercutting Don Juan's reputation by describing the deaths of two brothers who fought valiantly while other Christian soldiers looked on (curiously recalling somewhat tale 15 in *Count Lucanor*). As Yusuf ordered Algeciras turned over to the Christians, however, it was Don Juan who entered, displaying the castles and the rearing lions of Castile, and took control of the city in Alfonso's name. As he rode triumphantly beside the walls of Algeciras, his thoughts may have turned back thirty-five years to another siege of Algeciras, when as a young man he was accused of defection and treachery. The Juan Núñez at his side in 1344 was married to the granddaughter of the Infante Juan at his side in 1309. He must have felt a strangeness or loneliness observing the faces about him now.

The last four years of his life were not marked by the tempestuous activity of former years. His third wife, Blanca, had given him a son and a daughter. Agreement was reached to marry the son, Fernando Manuel, to the daughter of Ramón Berenguer, Jaime II's youngest son. These final years were spent in Garcimuñoz and on his lands in Murcia and Alicante. Jerónimo Zurita, Aragon's sixteenth-century historian, attests that Don Juan, unhappy with the little esteem he now commanded in Castile, sought to stir things up once more, secretly offering armed help to Aragon and Portugal if they chose to move against Alfonso XI and his productive mistress, La Guzmán (Giménez Soler, pp. 644–46); the latter two, Don Juan claimed (correctly), wished to marry off their many illegitimate children into other royal lines on the peninsula. Don Juan also warned of vague Castilian machinations against Aragon.[9] But at this late date, and in the face of an Alfonso XI in the fullness of his strength, such an aggressive proposal by Don Juan seems utterly incredible, a fantasy spun from senility.

Don Juan Manuel died on Friday, June 13, 1348.[10] The immediate circumstances of his death are not known. His body had definitely been taken to Peñafiel by mid 1351, since the Friars Preachers were then praying daily over his vault or *fuesa* for the repose of his soul. Argote de Molina reproduced in the sixteenth century, in the biography ("Vida del excelentísimo príncipe D. Juan Manuel") included in his *El Conde Lucanor* (Sevilla, 1575), the sepulcher's inscription in Peñafiel, which gave Córdoba as the place of his death and a date wrong by fourteen years; it is obvious that the epitaph was cut long after Don Juan's cadaver was laid to rest in the Dominican house he founded in Peñafiel, and where he had asked to be buried. No trace is to be seen of his tomb today in Peñafiel.

XIII *Juana Manuel; The Trastámara Dynasty Begins*

After the deaths of both Juan Manuel and Alfonso XI, the latter's concubine, Leonor de Guzmán, would seclude herself in Medina Sidonia, in fear of the sixteen-year-old Pedro I's advisers, and engineer a marriage between her eldest son, Enrique, and Don Juan's daughter Juana.[11] And now a series of events develops that might have caused Juan Manuel to turn in his grave. The long civil war of the fifties and sixties would culminate in the assassination of Pedro I in Duguesclin's tent in Montiel, and in a victory for the Trastámara faction. Enrique (as Enrique II) would be recognized as the first monarch of the bastard line of Trastámara. Juana Manuel, whose marriage to the illegitimate son of La Guzmán Don Juan would doubtless never have permitted, had become Queen of Castile. Her son Juan, named for her father, would be the second Trastámara to wear the crown, as Juan I.

One may imagine what Don Juan Manuel's reaction would have been, had he been told before he died that his grandson would be King of Castile.

CHAPTER 3

The Works of Don Juan Manuel

I MS 6376 and its "General" Prologue

A single fifteenth-century manuscript (No. 6376 of the Biblioteca Nacional in Madrid), filled with scribal flaws and lacunae, is the document that presents the bulk of Juan Manuel's prose. *Count Lucanor* is extant in four other manuscripts, all also from the fifteenth century, with the exception of one described by Juliá as from the sixteenth. The *Lucanor* manuscripts will be discussed further in Chapter 4. Barring the not impossible but unlikely discovery of some manuscript in the future, the totality of Juan Manuel's written work (see the list of his works, extant and lost, below), with the exception only of the *Lucanor* and the *Crónica abreviada*, would have been lost but for the survival of MS 6376.[1] It is obviously not an original omnibus master, as has sometimes been inadvertently claimed, nor is it even a copy of an original; its redaction comes at least a century later.

MS 6376 begins with the so-called "general" prologue in which Don Juan proclaims (he also calls this prologue a *protestación*), as he did earlier in the prefatory statement to *Count Lucanor,* that he is aware that he is being headstrong in undertaking to write such works as these; that he is aware of his own ignorance, which is such that today he has probably forgotten how to master proficiently a text [in Latin?]; but that the few copies that may be made of his works will certainly contain serious errors which he is helpless to prevent; hence this specially prepared volume, against which future copies may be checked.

The general prologue offers likewise, by way of illustration, the delightful story of the troubadour who, after hearing his best song dreadfully mauled by a shoemaker in both its lyrics and melody (*palabras e son*), takes a seat near the shop and listens a bit more to this gravel-voiced rendition. Then, his mind made

up, he slowly but deliberately picks up some scissors, cuts to
pieces every shoe in the stand, and calmly rides away. The
screaming cobbler goes after him, and eventually the case is
settled before the king to the great amusement of all. The well-
known plot is here typically amplified by Don Juan, who sets it
imaginatively and concretely in Perpignan in the reign of Jaume
I, and narrates it with the verve that makes his style unique in
its day.

II Don Juan Manuel's Personal Lists of His Works

In the prefatory statement to *Count Lucanor,* Don Juan
Manuel informs us that personally approved versions of his nine
works completed up to that time have been deposited in the
Dominican monastery of San Pablo in Peñafiel: *Crónica abreviada, Sabios, Cavallería, Libro del Infante, Cavallero et escudero,
Libro del Conde [Lucanor], Caça, Engeños, Cantares* (see the
listing and commentary below for full titles and works that have
more than one title). The *Lucanor* colophon indicates that this
work was finished in 1335. Then, at a later date, in the General
Prologue (in MS 6376) mentioned above, Don Juan provides a
second list of books that purports to constitute his written work
up to the time of the composition of this prologue. His personal
count of completed books at this later date totals (he says)
twelve: *Armas, Castigos et consejos, Estados* (= *Libro del Infante), Cavallero et escudero, Cavallería, Crónica abreviada,
Crónica conplida, Egennos, Caça, Cantigas* (= *Cantares), Reglas
commo se deven trobar.* The latter list given by Don Juan plainly
provides only eleven titles, but the announced total (twelve)
makes it clear that the startling omission of *El Conde Lucanor*
was not intended. The author's count in his second list, nevertheless, is incorrect, since he omits one work (*Sabios*) that he
claimed earlier in the *Lucanor* listing.

There are, then, four new titles in Don Juan's second or General Prologue list that can be added to the nine of the earlier
enumeration in the *Lucanor: Armas, Castigos et consejos* (= *Libro
infinido), Crónica conplida,* and *Reglas.* Attempts to ascertain
the total number of this author's works, however, are further
complicated by the fact that MS 6376 contains a work that does
not appear on either of Don Juan's lists: an essay on the Assumption generally given the short title *Tratado de la Asunción,* but

also often called *Tractado en que se prueba por razón que Sancta María está en cuerpo et alma en paraýso.* The nine works of the *Lucanor* listing plus the four new items from the *prólogo general,* plus also the Assumption piece, make a minimal total of at least fourteen works authored by Don Juan Manuel whose titles are known:

Crónica cumplida	*(Complete History)*
Libro de los sabios	*(Book of the Philosophers)*
Libro de la cavallería	*(Book on Knighthood)*
Libro de los engeños	*(Book on Mechanized Warfare)*
Libro de los cantares	*(Book of Poems)*
Libro de las reglas	*(Art of Poetic Composition)*
commo se deven trovar	
Crónica abreviada	*(Outline History)*
Libro del cavallero et	*(Book about the Knight and*
del escudero	*the Apprentice-Knight)*
Libro infinido	*(The Unfinished Book)*
El Conde Lucanor	*(Count Lucanor)*
Libro de las armas	*(Book on the Coat of Arms)*
Libro de los estados	*(Book on the Plan of Society)*
Libro de la caza	*(Book on Hunting)*
Tractado de la Asunción	*(Essay on the Assumption)*

No known copies of the first six works in this list exist. They are probably lost forever, leaving extant the other eight; the situation could easily have been much worse. No chronology of composition is to be read into the listing above. Don Juan himself apparently displays no concern for such chronology in either of his lists, but this is perhaps something that might be looked into more closely. The titles of several of his works vary, both in the words of Juan Manuel himself and in later redactions: the *Libro infinido* is more often called *Libro de castigos et de consejos (Instruction and Counsel);* the *Libro de las armas* is the *Libro de las tres razones (The Three Topics);* either the *Crónica cumplida* or the *abdeviada* is called the *Crónica de España* by Gonzalo Argote de Molina in his sixteenth-century princeps edition of *El Conde Lucanor;* the *Libro de cantares* may be *de cantigas;* the *Libro de los estados* is the *Libro del Infante;* etc.

In most scholarly accounts of Don Juan Manuel there is mention of the copies of his works, listed in *Count Lucanor,* that the author claims to have deposited in Peñafiel; Manueline critics are likewise fond of speculating about the nature and the disappearance of these copies. These personally corrected manuscripts, placed for safekeeping in 1335 (or shortly before that date) with the friars in the Dominican house founded by Don Juan himself, are an indication of the author's concern over the carelessness and mutilation that occur in the process of copying and reproducing works; he seeks to preserve the pristine originals.[2] Questions are raised, however, by the existence of the chronologically later General Prologue and its longer list of works: Is this prologue an indication that Juan Manuel ordered at this later date new master copies produced of all his works written up to that time? Or is it simply a preface of sorts that he thought proper at that time to include as an introduction to the then larger master tome of his works? He repeats, as we have seen, his concern mentioned earlier in the *Lucanor* over the unavoidable scribal errors in the copying process, and he illustrates his point with the tale of the troubadour and the cobbler. There is no reference, however, in the General Prologue to the Peñafiel foundation, and it is explicitly stated that a single omnibus volume contains approved versions of all his works.

It appears likely that the General Prologue follows *Count Lucanor* by some half dozen years. And since the single surviving manuscript of most of his works contains a treatise (the Assumption piece) omitted in both of Don Juan's personal lists, a treatise that is probably among the last things that he wrote, it has even been thought possible that there existed as many as three master collections of the author's works. It is important to remember, of course, that MS 6376 was copied in the fifteenth century, perhaps a hundred years after the original master versions were corrected and polished by their author.[3] The discovery of the (or a) master collection of Don Juan Manuel's works would indeed constitute a decisive and welcome event in Manueline scholarship.

III *The Chronology of the Works of Don Juan Manuel*

Baist and Giménez Soler, relying heavily on internal evidence, have proposed tentative chronologies of Juan Manuel's works. Although they disagree on the historical and hunting books and at certain points in their suggested datings, there is substantial agreement on a general ordering of the major works that coincides with an earlier chronology proposed by Amador de los Ríos.[4] What follows, then, is an approximate and tentative chronology of six of Don Juan's works based on the three scholars' indications:

Cavallero et Escudero	mid 1320's
Estados	completed very early 1330's
Lucanor	early 1330's; finished 1335
Infinido	mid 1330's
Prólogo general	late 1330's or early 1340's
Asunción	early 1340's

IV   The Lost Works; The Histories; Other Documents

Libro de la cavallería (Knighthood). Don Juan himself provides occasional indications in *Estados* (I, 67, 85, 90, 91) of the contents of this lost work on the duties, etc., of the chivalric tradition, composed early (probably before 1326) in the fifteen-to twenty-year period of his life during which he devoted some time to serious literary endeavor.

Libro de los sabios (Philosophers). Possibly a collection of proverbs with commentary, in the tradition of wisdom literature or, in the view of some, a work of philosophic or religious discussions among several learned people, in the manner of Ramón Llull.

Libro de los engeños (War Machines). Greatly lamented by military historians especially is the loss of this work, glimpses of whose contents may possibly be got in certain chapters in *Estados* (I, 77, e.g.): the technique of defending the areas of an outer wall not under the protective cover of a tower by swinging massive boulders retained by ropes onto attacking troops who seek to scale or excavate.

The Poetic Works: The recovery of the book on the art of composition would make it the earliest such treatise in Spanish literature; hence the seriousness of this loss. Commentators at times feel the urge to make guesses concerning the nature of Juan Manuel's lost book of poems, and some, after digesting the distichs in the *Lucanor*, are rude enough to suggest that perhaps the disappearance of his poetry constitutes no devastating blow to Spanish literature. J. M. Blecua, on the other hand, wonders (ed. *Libro infinido,* 1952, p. vii) if it could have been a work similar to the *Book of Good Love.*

The Histories: The author lists his *Outline History* in the *Lucanor* prologue, and both works are then claimed in the general prologue. The *Crónica cumplida,* or longer chronicle, has not been found, although it was thought formerly, and apparently mistakenly, by some that a brief list of events in Latin for the years 1274–1329,[5] prepared evidently at Juan Manuel's order or for his use, was actually the missing work. The extant history is a product of the early period (1320's) in his writing career; it summarizes his uncle's *Estoria de España.*

An extraordinarily rich corpus of letters, documents of every kind, testaments, legal papers, etc., either by or about Don Juan Manuel, exists, due primarily to the rich archives of the Crown of Aragon. Don Juan's personal correspondence itself constitutes a major bloc of writings that the student interested in the man or his century can ill afford to overlook. One may well wonder what impressions of fourteenth-century peninsular history (and of the personality of Don Juan Manuel) would be today, were it not for the presence of this veritable storehouse of information.[6]

CHAPTER 4

Castilian Prose Fiction Comes of Age

I *Eastern Tale and Western Didacticism*

THE practice, as in Juan Manuel's *Conde Lucanor*, of using
tales, fables, short narratives, etc., as *exempla* for the purpose
of pointing up a lesson and illustrating and enhancing moral
advice is considered so basic a medieval technique that sight may
be lost of the fact that the medieval world either borrows or
inherits from Greco-Roman, biblical, Patristic, and oriental
sources, not only the technique, but a great portion of the narrative and proverbial material itself. And what is perhaps unduly
emphasized, with respect to medieval western Europe and its
inheritance of this large corpus of borrowed stories, is their use
as didactic materials, to the point of slighting these age-old
narratives as pure entertainment. Obviously they were used for
instructional purposes, yet these stories did not live such healthy
lives from generation to generation primarily because they were
found effective in improving the morals of mankind, but because
people liked to hear them, and retell them, again and again.
This view in no way negates the profound influence of the scrip-
tural use of the concrete parable on such similar illustrative techniques employed by artists and authors throughout the Middle
Ages.

In the Europe of the twelfth and thirteenth centuries, a Europe
at the peak of a religious and cultural upsurge of major proportions, the task of copying collections of tales was vigorously pursued. Each *speculum, corpus, summa,* etc., sought to harvest a
crop greater than that of its predecessor, and the early major
collections were with good reason made in Latin so that their
audience would be international. The possibility of using such
narrative materials to add both zest and body to sleep-inducing
sermons appealed to the clergy, whose needs, especially those
of the mendicant orders making a specialty of preaching to the

man in the street, were soon satisfied with ready-made and easy-to-consult reference compendiums.

Important supply routes for these tales had found their way westward from points east: India, Greece, Persia, North Africa. Spain, with its southern regions occupied by the Moslems, would play a major role in the redaction of some of this material, and in the decisive matter of readying it for transmission to the rest of Christian Europe. A precedent was established early in Toledo, where a group of translators, composed of Christians, Moslems, and Jews, had been organized under the aegis of an archbishop after that city was retaken by the Christians in 1085. Apparently often the Christian scholar with classical training would compose his work in Latin, basing it on a rough draft in Castilian that had been translated from the Arabic text; the Romance version, oral in some cases, was supplied by a Jewish scholar who could thus serve as intermediary between the Christian knowing no Arabic and the Moslem knowing no Latin.[1] A great increase in such activity occurred in the thirteenth century, and in this fashion an awareness not only of the tales, but of the manner in which they were structurally linked in fictional frames, spread through Christian Spain.

The use of a thread of continuing dialogue, a unifying thread that reappears after each tale in order to introduce the next one, was one such convenient, although at times quite loose, frame. In the *Libro de los engaños (Book of Deceitful Ways)*, for example, the son falsely accused of the attempted seduction of a concubine has his execution postponed as one learned adviser after another tells the king (the boy's father) a misogynous story he believes appropriate to the occasion. This latter work, belonging to a branch of the much-traveled *Book of Sindibad*, and the *Calila e Digna*, a collection of tales making great use of animal protagonists and reproducing in part the Indian *Panchatantra*, are the first collections of *exempla* that appear in Spanish. The immediate predecessors of these books of oriental stories and lore in their Spanish versions were Arabic versions. Translated at the request of Castilian princes in the middle of the thirteenth century, they stand out in any history of prose fiction in the peninsula, yet a balanced overview of the situation must be maintained by keeping in mind the presence and availability of abundant international collections in Latin throughout the age.

On the peninsula itself, a very early and influential collection of thirty-four tales in Latin, the *Disciplina Clericalis*, had been assembled in the twelfth century by Pedro Alfonso, a converted Jewish physician from Huesca who was to enjoy a remarkable career in international circles.[2] Many of the stories repeated in this work are part of that huge store of tales already at that time so well known throughout western Europe that many should be considered traditional, popular motifs. The "Story of the Half-Friend," for example, of remote oriental origin, is an Eastern tale adapted to the bare Latin of Pedro Alfonso's work; it circulates around western Europe through this and other Latin, as well as Romance, collections, and will be utilized by Juan Manuel in tale 48 in *Count Lucanor*. The loose frames used to bind these groups of tales together vary: in Pedro Alfonso a father is trying to educate his son in the vicissitudes of life, the virtues of prudence, etc. As will be seen shortly, Juan Manuel will use a similarly slanted network of dialogue in his collection of *exempla* called *Count Lucanor*. Other collections of tales, in either Latin or Spanish, go unmentioned here; there should be little doubt that, given Juan Manuel's personality and interests, he found access to as many as were available.

II Count Lucanor: *The Author's Plan*

"And Don Johan finished it in Salmerón, on Monday the 12th of June, in 1335." Thus does Don Juan Manuel, in his castle in reconquered territory in Murcia, complete the work that has been the basis for his literary reputation. *El Conde Lucanor (Count Lucanor)*, a collection of fifty-one didactic units linked in a typical Eastern frame of running dialogue between two people (here lord and advisor), will also be his only work to reach, with the passing of time, great numbers of readers. It does so very early, through its publication by Gonzalo Argote de Molina in 1575 in Sevilla, and through another edition in 1642 in Madrid. But perhaps the fact that this book became the only work of medieval Castilian literature known firsthand by Golden Age writers was due to the numbers of manuscripts which we may surmise were copied in the fourteenth and fifteenth centuries, thus making it likely that a copy would attract the attention of an enterprising antiquarian like Argote.[3] The utilization and awareness of the stories in *Count Lucanor* in major figures (Lope,

Calderón, and Gracián, for example) in Spain's Golden Age attest to the popularity of the collection during the sixteenth and seventeenth centuries.

Count Lucanor is without argument from any quarter Juan Manuel's major accomplishment as a writer. Since it is his only work that has received a substantial amount of critical attention, his stature as a signal figure of importance in the development of medieval Castilian prose is due largely to this single masterpiece. The title *Count Lucanor* is the one that has been traditionally used by most editors, beginning with Argote de Molina; it was never used by Juan Manuel, who names his work the *Book of Exemplos of Count Lucanor and Patronio* in his opening remarks, and refers to it as the *Book of Patronio* in the *Libro infinido*. It is a work in five parts. The first part, quite detachable from the much shorter, final pieces, constitutes by far the bulk of the text. It begins with a very brief opening statement, followed in turn by a prologue that introduces the body proper of the first part's text. The latter then consists of fifty-one didactic units that are in themselves each carefully organized around the core of a brief tale, fable, or historical anecdote. The organized arrangement of these several elements and the step-by-step procedure utilized by Don Juan are characteristic only in a secondary way of the authoritarian and political nature of the man himself, a noble much given to keeping his affairs in a clearly stated and neatly ordered fashion; primarily, this arrangement of his materials in well-defined and interlocking blocks (even though each unit has an independence within the whole) is a design consciously imitative and typically reminiscent of the patterns found in collections of fictional tales from the East that for more than a century had found acceptance in Christian Spain.

In his pre-prologue statement, Juan Manuel states that he has selected the *exemplos* in this collection carefully so as to provide his readers with the most profitable lessons possible for the benefit of their well-being both in this life and the one to come.[4] It is often pointed out that Juan Manuel, both here and in the illustrative tales to follow, is much more interested in the material side of life on earth than he is in the salvation of his soul; he mentions here three aspects of the former, to a single reference to the latter. There is, however, no dichotomy in his thinking, as has been shown in recent studies.[5] To extract a value judgment, where none was intended, from a mere enumeration of the ways in which one might profitaby use his work is to misinterpret him, to read into his words a categorization that he did not wish to make. Don Juan believes that the broad range of human activity covered in his many tales is such that practically any problem that one might face will find a reasonable parallel (hence, solution) somewhere in this work.

His next point is highly indicative of the man's punctilious nature and, for a medieval writer, quite fussy regard for what later and presumably more learned readers will have to say of his work: He rejects, in a blanket assertion, any and all criticisms of his language and style from readers who have only examined second- and third-hand copies sure to contain misspellings and incorrect, confused phrasing leading to misinterpretation. He does not want such carelessness and ignorance attributed to him, as, he says, often happens to other writers. He will, however, accept criticism from those who have taken the trouble to look over the personally corrected master copies of his works in the care of the friars at the Dominican house in Peñafiel, an establishment built at Juan Manuel's expense beginning in 1318. Such adverse criticism of stylistic detail may be directed at his *mengua de entendimiento,* here meaning "lack of broad, formal education," but not against his *entençión,* i.e., imputing to him any carelessness or shoddiness in attitude or aim in the way in which he went about preparing this work. Don Juan's concern over the reproduction of his writings may be opposed to the lack of such awareness in other medieval Romance authors and is a trait that markedly characterizes his literary personality. Few manuals of literature fail to contrast his touchiness on this subject with the free-wheeling attitude of his contemporary, Juan Ruiz, who in jongleur fashion invites his audience to add verses to his *Book of Good Love* and to change it for the better, if it thinks that it can.

In closing his short introductory statement, he includes a list of his works and states that his purpose is to reach a public that has not benefited from the wisdom that one receives from a substantial amount of formal education. He himself, he repeats, is without such training and therefore has composed this book in Castilian (i.e., not in Latin). This should be a clear indication, he believes, of its true purpose. Although much of what he writes here is easily related to oft-stated topoi in the Middle Ages, the sentiments expressed appear to be strongly felt; he will repeat them elsewhere. He is satisfied with what he has done; he asks only that others understand what he is doing, and especially, to what end.

In the prologue proper, Don Juan stresses the utilitarian goals in his work. His book does not pretend to theorize via subtle philosophical nuances. It offers plain and practical advice; its author has already pointed to his utilitarian rule of thumb (*los enxiemplos más aprovechosos*) in the selection of materials. That basic tenet of medieval artistic endeavor, the presentation of a beneficial message in a form attractive to its public, receives clear expression here. The truth must be made palatable, and Don Juan uses the example of medicine that operates more efficiently when sugarcoated. The example-giving tales inserted from time to time, therefore, will provide profitable advice for every reader, even for those who do not seek such advice and read only to entertain themselves. In customary fashion, he invokes God's help in the task of composition. Should anyone be pleased by the aesthetic qualities of the text or profit from its lessons, the author asks that the credit be ultimately reserved for his Creator.

A consistent structural plan runs through all fifty-one individual units: Count Lucanor, a wealthy landowning lord at the maturity of his power, describes a personal problem then facing him and requests advice from his counselor Patronio.[6] The latter complies, illustrating his advice with a story that is the core of each didactic frame. The brief tale is what the reader is eagerly anticipating; it is the artistic vehicle for a kernel of wise advice, the sugarcoating on the pill. The unit then continues in the third person with a statement that the Count, satisfied with the counsel, acted accordingly and benefited therefrom. A shift disconcerting to the modern reader occurs when the author suddenly introduces himself into the reader's train of thought. In the third person he announces that Don Johan, finding the *exemplo* of good quality, ordered it copied as a part of this collection. Such third-person references to himself are a common feature of Juan Manuel's style.

To make his lesson even more palatable the author then reduces it to a brief memorizable version, couching the bare moral in a rhymed couplet of uninspired, prosaic verse.[7] Practicing a typical synthesis or *simplificatio,* Don Juan produces the only extant examples of his poetic art, since no copy of his book of verse has been found. So stilted at times that one suspects that the verse was mangled as it was copied, his poetic technique is nevertheless not without interest for the student of the history of versification on the peninsula.[8]

There are here no references by Don Juan to sources utilized, or to "authorities' (such as those thrown out by Juan Ruiz) who are supposed to serve as supports for his contentions; to find noteworthy the lack of such references is to fail to understand the essential nature of this work and the intent of its author. His concern is for a polished, refined product of which he is proud, and which he considers (and expects others to consider) essentially his own work, since he has, as he says in the prologue, "composed this book to the best of my ability, using as elegant a style as possible." He wishes to receive credit for those original hues and shades added in his retelling of these tales; he is of course aware that the bare narratives themselves, and even the historical anecdotes that he is fond of reshaping, may be quite familiar in many cases to both educated and uneducated in the fourteenth century. It is the "how," not the "what," that matters most. Don Juan thinks of this book as an original work; it is original, in the sense that this adjective has in the fourteenth century.

III   *And the Count Asked Him to Tell That Story . . .*

The tale at the core of each unit is introduced with a proposal from Patronio that he illustrate his requested counsel by means of a story. In given cases, such as units 15 and 50, Juan Manuel shows himself especially concerned with a particular problem and has Patronio comment on certain psychological or personal attitudes before going on to tell the tale whose story clarifies and establishes on firm ground the final word of advice to follow.

The fifty-one units may be grouped according to various criteria: possible specific or general sources, the psychological nature of the problems posed and the advice received, the thematics running through the tales (Moslem settings, use or absence or degree of local color, Castilian history, animal apologues, e.g.), etc. It is impossible to determine Juan Manuel's immediate sources; Don Juan himself may not have been able to recall specifically where he heard or read the gist or outline of a given tale. In any case, many of these stories were the stories everyone told in his day; they were part of a substantial storehouse of tales to be used and repeated as the occasion arose. Don Juan may well have heard many of them narrated on more than one occasion. It would be strange, however, were the *exemplum*-collections assembled under Dominican auspices for use in sermons *not* utilized by the author, since it is likely such collections were readily available among his Dominican friends in Peñafiel and in other houses of Friars Preachers elsewhere. A number of the tales (4, 6, 11, 18, 36, 45, 49) could definitely have been read in some known Dominican compilation of either *exempla* or complete sermons, or in other pious works by Dominicans.[9] This does not mean that they could not be heard or read elsewhere, but the vogue of the preachers' collections must be given prime consideration, especially in view of the fact that others (14, 31) are possibly tinged with Dominican influence. The 144 pages of end-notes to Hermann Knust's edition of this work, published posthumously in 1900, are richly suggestive of possible sources. M. R. Lida de Malkiel has likewise made some pertinent observations on the relations of these tales with others in the classical and medieval worlds. Others who have attempted comparative studies of Juan Manuel's material and talk of "influences" and "sources" have not always fared so successfully. The tales (15, 16, 37) springing from anecdotes chronicled in recent Castilian histories have for obvious reasons aroused considerable interest.

A number of Juan Manuel's tales (minimally, 20, 21, 30, 32, 35, 41, 46, and 47, but to these should be added possibly several others) were *apparently* not circulating in the early fourteenth century in any Romance or Latin version. Arabic sources for these may seem on the surface a possibility, and some have made a case for Juan Manuel's "oriental" outlook and tastes, his preference for Eastern attitudes, his willingness to be influenced by Moslem cultural postures, matched by an unwillingness to be seduced by the classical influences of the Greco-Roman world.[10] After everything has been said, nevertheless, one is left with the impression that not very much has been said. Since many of the Eastern tales current and available in the Castile of Juan Manuel do not circulate as such, but in westernized versions, or in Dominican retellings, or in Alfonsine molds (*Libro de los engaños, Calila e Digna*), it could be dangerous to stress with far-reaching categorical statements the place of Arabic influence in the tales and the psychology of *Count Lucanor,* other than to say simply that the author used certain stories that were oriental in origin and certain tales with oriental settings, something that would have been difficult for him not to do. This does not mean that it is not patently worthwhile to examine other earlier and contemporary versions of the tales that he tells; striking insights into his art can be thus obtained. What can be said is that Juan Manuel was attracted, possibly to a degree greater than many other Castilian magnates of his time, to Moslem traditions and lore, and that he doubtless expressed interest in Eastern fictional apologues whenever and however he came across them. There should be no mystery as to how he found access to such narratives. He could have heard them time and again in oral Romance versions from many sources, including his Jewish and other bilingual advisers; he could have heard them in third-, fourth-, and fifth-hand versions.

It is likewise of no great use in this respect to dwell upon the probability of Juan Manuel's being able to read Arabic. There is no firm indication of any kind that this could be the case, and there probably never will be. Of course he knew some Arabic; monolingual American soldiers stationed in Germany know some German, too. The strains of *mudéjar* life coloring the Castile in which he lived made it impossible not to know some Arabic, and a great part of his life was furthermore spent on the frontier, in Murcia and across Granada's Vega to Sevilla, at times in direct dealings with Moslem emissaries. Lida de Malkiel has shown that Don Juan made use of a respectable reading knowledge of Latin, despite his protestations of lay ignorance in this *lingua franca* of the educated medieval man. A century earlier, Berceo could similarly protest his ignorance even as he ploughed through the Latin text of a saint's life before him; such statements are a literary device common to many medieval writers.

And now that the prologue is finished, I shall begin at this point my book proper, in which a nobleman and his adviser are carrying on a conversation. And the noble's name is Count Lucanor, and that of his adviser, Patronio.

(Prólogo del *Conde Lucanor*)

EXEMPLO 1. "A King and His Favorite"

This well-knit story of triple deception—the King by certain lesser advisers, the favorite by the King, and then the King again by his favorite—is told, with considerable differences, in the Greek version of the Barlaam and Josaphat legend, as Moldenhauer observes in his study of the latter theme on the peninsula.[11] Don Juan may have had at hand some version of the Barlaam story (he also uses the frame of this work in *Estados*), despite the remote possibility that the popularity of the Barlaam frame and its *exempla* was such that they had become folklore through constant repetition orally and in other *exempla* collections. Juan Manuel's colorful retelling of this tale of a King who tests his favorite's loyalty is done in typical straightforward fashion and is superior to other versions, especially with its description of the presence in the favorite's house of a "captive, a wise and brilliant philosopher," who advises his master to shave his head and beard, and dress in the rags and nail-patched shoes of a begging pilgrim, in order to deceive his King. Knust (p. 299) observes another version of this test-of-loyalty theme in the *Legenda Aurea* that derives from the Greek *Barlaam.* Juan Manuel's interest in the theme of deception, the people who perpetrate it, and its consequences, will run unabated through many more tales.

EXEMPLO 2. "A Well-Intentioned Man and His Son"

The widely known Eastern story of the man and lad who are criticized no matter what they do with their beast, walk beside it or ride it, is told here to illustrate the idea that one must act as his conscience dictates. One must be his own master: *non dexes de lo fazer por reçelo de dicho de las gentes.*

EXEMPLO 3. "King Richard's Leap"

The old tale of the hermit who, near the end of a life of penance, seeks a promise of Paradise from his Lord is here splendidly retold by Don Juan. Upon hearing that his fate will be that of Richard the Lion-Heart, whose reputation for thievery and breaking people's heads was notorious, he despairs. His fears vanish, however, as in a story within the outer tale he hears of Richard's repentance for past wrongs and his famous leap, armed and on horseback, from a Crusader vessel into the teeth of the enemy forces, thereby leading his men to a victory pleasing in the sight of God. The sources of this tale, whose original lesson was the exaltation of the hermit's life of deprivation, have been commented on profusely, and the tale itself has received generous attention from more than a few critics. The ideas in this story have been often considered prized mirrors of the author's personal creed of life before death and his private agonies about life after death.

EXEMPLO 4. "The Dying Genoese"

In this brief tale, whose source for the author was probably a Dominican preachers' guide, the *genovés* on the point of death assembles his friends and his great riches in a pleasant seaside spot overlooking his merchant fleet. He considers the many reasons he has to go on living, and asks his soul if it wishes to leave behind all these material and spiritual comforts for an uncertain future elsewhere. If you do, the dying man informs his soul, addressing it directly, then you can go straight to hell for all I care. The lesson dictated by Patronio here, curiously enough, is not to risk present comforts in order to undertake some vague enterprise urged on one by so-called friends. In the dry Latin versions of this tale from Dominican sources (Jean Hérolt, *Promptuarium exemplorum*; John Bromyard, *Summa praedicantium*: both preachers' guides or *exemplum*-collections) quoted by Knust (pp. 307–8), the protagonists are dull, nameless misers or usurers. Thus Juan Manuel particularizes and enlivens his rendition even in this brief one-page scene: the Croesus here is a gilt-laden merchant of Genoa, relaxing sumptuously at his ocean villa and in a playful mood to tease his very soul. The moralizing, mnemonic capsule that completes the unit is not a couplet here but a folk proverb (and distinguished as such from the learned sayings in the apendices): *Quien bien se siede non se lieve* (If you go looking for trouble, you'll find it). Don Juan describes this as something the "old women of Castile like to repeat," and it is easy to imagine that a man with such a tendency to moralize would be fond of pithy sayings, be they folk or learned.[12]

EXEMPLO 5. "The Fox and the Crow"

The extraordinary popularity in the West of this Eastern animal fable found in Phaedrus is well attested. Juan Manuel's enterprising fox, who by systematic and logical reasoning coolly coaxes the cheese from the crow's mouth, has been contrasted by Menéndez Pidal with the screaming, tempestuous characterization found in Juan Ruiz.[13]

EXEMPLO 6. "The Swallow's Warning"

This unadorned tale with its simple message of caution (nip trouble in the bud before the situation is completely out of hand) is likewise a fable of Eastern provenance whose wide-ranging popularity is profusely annotated by Knust (pp. 313–16). This is the story of the swallow who unsuccessfully urges his feathered friends to destroy the flax when first sown in the fields so that it may never be harvested and spun into treacherous nets and traps. The temptation to see a reference to some specific incident, in vague admonitions such as the one provided here, is difficult to resist for readers in search of something to search for. As is his custom, the author here has first simply hit upon a tale that he wants to use, and has composed the unit around it, including the Count's presentation of a personal problem that is supposed to generate the succeeding narrative. Often this presentation, couched in vague, general terms, appears artificially contrived. The story of the swallow here is introduced by the Count's statement to Patronio that he has heard that his neighbors are planning to give him some trouble.

EXEMPLO 7. "Doña Truhana and the Pot of Honey"

The Eastern story of the misfortune that befalls the vain dreamer, who loses the little he or she has while imagining future riches, is known best as "The Milkmaid" in its immense progeny in the West, including many English versions (Knust, pp. 316–18). In the *Calila e Digna* version (ed. J. E. Keller and R. W. Linker, 1967, pp. 252–54), which some assume perforce was Juan Manuel's source, the protagonist is a hermit who, in the course of a dream of future wealth to accrue from a pot of honey and butter hanging on his bed's headboard, moves violently and smashes the pot, its contents drenching his head.

[74]

EXEMPLO 8. "The Sick Man and His Liver"

The curious problem that the Count offers here is how to deal with people who come with requests at inopportune times, people whom one would like to help, given other circumstances. The answer is clear in an amusing, sharply pointed scene in this story, with its interesting medical sidelight, of a suffering individual and the surgery that he must endure. A stranger wanders up in the course of the operation (in which the wretch has had his liver removed temporarily [!] for medicinal cleansing) and asks the conscious patient if he could use a little bit of his liver to feed his cat.

EXEMPLO 9. "The Horse and the Lion"

The author touches up with concrete detail the old story of the animals who, despite their hate, find it convenient to become allies in the face of an enemy too powerful for either of them individually. The story is provided with an intriguing locale, Tunis, and an interesting figure from late thirteenth-century Castilian history is thrown into the tale in an apparently offhand way, as Juan Manuel goes about polishing some of the first short prose tales in medieval Europe notably marked with a writer's personal style. The Infante Enrique, fourth son of Fernando III, a wily schemer whose extraordinary life included banishment to Africa by his brother, Alfonso X, and an unsuccessful attempt by the King of Tunis to feed him to lions, is an appropriate person to be used as a background figure here, in view of his North African adventures.[14] Variations on the theme of this *exemplo* ("United we stand, divided we fall") appear in several medieval Latin source books; in the *Gesta Romanorum* and Bromyard's *Summa praedicantium,* the protagonists are dogs allied against a wolf. Patronio's final moralizing strikes a note struck often whenever Juan Manuel philosophizes on the vicissitudes in the life of a man of his social rank: One must put up with a lot of garbage from his relatives and neighbors to insure that he is not ultimately destroyed by his enemies.

EXEMPLO 10. "The Man Who Felt Sorry for Himself"

In his *Life Is a Dream* (I, 2) Calderón appears to have read his *Lucanor* by retelling in a ten-line strophe this apologue of the man who, once rich but now reduced to eating a meager ration of seeds (lupines) and believing himself the most miserable creature alive, observes another man tracing his steps and happy to eat the discarded shells.

EXEMPLO 11. "The Sorcerer of Toledo"

In this well-structured tale, Don Juan Manuel reaches the highest level of his art, manipulating neglected facets of time and reality as finely honed stylistic devices in a superb recasting of an old story of ingratitude. The usual qualities of compactness and lineal directness in his customary single-track narrative chain are present, but joined to these is an awareness of the added depth a story can have if it can capture, for the imaginative, receptive reader, an essential detail or two of the outer reality and inner essence of the moment in time and space that it seeks to depict. We are at that point, in the range of artistic creation in Don Juan Manuel, at which he, though not losing sight altogether of his didactic aim, finds himself devoting much greater attention to the artistic shaping of his narrative, aware of what a few original strokes can add to the telling.

The setting is Toledo, the Toledo of the low Middle Ages, the mere mention of whose name to the outsider brought on images of necromancers and their astonishing magical arts. Few tales in the *Lucanor* have specific locales; this one takes place one evening in the extraordinary house of the soothsayer Don Illán, whose fame in these forbidden practices has attracted an ecclesiastic from distant Santiago. The latter, a man of substantial position already in his capacity as chapter master of the Galician cathedral, eagerly and improperly is seeking instruction in the black arts. He would first meet the great master of Toledo, appropriately, in "a room quite secluded from the rest of the house," yet he was to be received hospitably, well fed, and generously housed. His host, however, with a splendidly mysterious touch, as if already piercing the transparency of the ecclesiastic's thoughts, had asked when they first met that he not mention the reason for his trip until they had enjoyed a midday meal. The afternoon and evening are then spent in serious discussions, with promises by the churchman of eternal obedience in order to assuage the sorcerer's expressed doubts that a man of his position would be truly grateful after acquiring the diviner's secrets.

With strikingly modern technique, Juan Manuel now permits

the plane of reality in which these events are operating to slip away subtly and imperceptibly. Time stops, and a chain of occurrences triggered in the mind of the Toledan master envelopes that extraordinary study chamber, "so deep in the earth's depths that it seemed that they were beneath the Tagus," a chamber to which master and neophyte had descended down "a remarkably well-carved stone staircase." In order to be able later to key the passage from time-marked reality to timelessness and back, the author has the sorcerer order a girl to prepare partridges for supper, but not to roast them until so requested; this occurs just before the subterranean descent, thus quietly, unobtrusively, setting up a psychic curtain in the ecclesiastic's mind (as well as in the reader's) that can be triggered to fall later with a sudden order that it was time to put the partridges on the fire. With an imaginary snap of his fingers the author will at the crucial moment do for the reader what the sorcerer does for his student.

The extratemporal sequence of events involves, naturally, permitting the cleric from Santiago to reveal his true nature, which turns out to be one of uncommon ingratitude. This sequence is ignited with a felicitous touch as Juan Manuel has the two men in the well-appointed chamber turn to examining the strange books that will reveal for the neophyte the mysteries of divination. As the selection of texts proceeds, this chain of activity is broken suddenly as the door opens and they look up to see two men bearing a letter. The amount of detailed description (with the staircase and room, for example), though seemingly minimal, is noteworthy here because of its absence as a rule elsewhere. An apparent succession of promotions moves the cleric upward in the hierarchy, and it is as he imagines that he is Pope that he turns on his benefactor, threatening him now (a charming turnabout) with the charge of heresy and witchcraft, and ordering him to leave without partaking of any available food. At that exact moment, the sorcerer states that if such be the case, he then has no recourse but to dine on his ready-to-roast partridges. A final line provides a delightful twist as the sorcerer with great good humor observes that, under the circumstances, it would be most improper for the churchman, who now is embarrassed and speechless as he sees his true self revealed, to eat his share of the partridges now roasting.

Easily acclaimed the favorite by the critical attention that it has received, the core of this tale was probably borrowed from similar stories in several earlier Latin collections, Dominican and otherwise.[15] Knust's suggestive remarks (especially pp. 324–29) have generated interesting but inconclusive speculation on a possible connection between the cavernous study of Don Illán and the legendary cave of Hercules. Illán was apparently the name of a Toledan family with a reputation in the field of black magic as early as the twelfth century. Azorín and Borges have written twentieth-century recastings of this tale that do not diminish one's appreciation of the original.[16] Of the Golden Age and subsequent adaptations of either the totality or parts of the story of Don Illán, Ruiz de Alarcón's *La prueba de las promesas* (*Testing the Value of Promises*) is outstanding. The Baroque moral philosopher, Baltasar Gracián, in view of his customary praise for Juan Manuel, naturally flatters the latter's encompassing an instructive lesson in so attractive a package as this tale.[17]

EXEMPLO 12. "The Fox and the Rooster"

The threat of attack and the psychological atmosphere preceding possible war is discussed by Patronio (or Juan Manuel), who in contemporary terms would be a believer in the domino theory of the piecemeal destruction of the whole if a firm stand is not made, in person, at one's most distant stretch of rightfully owned land. The rooster is destroyed ultimately only because the fox discovers that he can be made to panic. Walled fortifications, we are told, can be taken in two ways only, by scaling and/or excavating, and these are generally never successful unless the besieged become rumor-ridden and panic sets in.

EXEMPLO 13. "The Trapper and the Partridges"

Another Eastern fable built on a prayerful proverb: God save me from those who say that they are sorry that they have to do me so much harm. The wind makes the trapper's eyes water as he kills and removes the birds caught in his nets. One of the birds, in a lively bit of dialogue, screeches to her friends that their murderer in his sorrow really pities them. A wiser bird repeats the mentioned proverb. A Spanish version of Eude de Cheriton's *Fabulae*, the *Libro de los gatos* (ed. J. E. Keller, 1958, p. 39), has an earlier telling of this tale that is anticlerical in its moralizing: The hunter simply has weak, watering eyes, like those of hypocritical prelates whose eyes water mechanically as they pray away.

EXEMPLO 14. "St. Dominic and the Usurer"

A doubly interesting story both in the author's manipulation of the *exemplum* of the usurer's rotting heart and in its moralizing on the subject of wealth. Don Juan Manuel, accused at times of being obsessively greedy, is here a man disturbed by the "problem" of wealth. He takes pains to underscore (through Patronio) the unequivocal pressures a man of his station faces if he is to carry out his mission in society. Wealth, then, is absolutely necessary. It must be amassed constantly, but not so blindly as to obscure one's other equally and more important responsibilities. This apologue stands out since it is not Eastern, but was formed in the West around the admonishment in Matthew VI: 21 and Luke XII: 34 that a man's heart can be found in what he treasures most. It receives a sprightly telling in Sancho IV's *Castigos (Counsel) y documentos* (ed. A. Rey, 1952, Chap. VII), in which the avaricious character has contracted a mania for running his fingers through his gold that is so pernicious that it has to be satisfied daily. While one day thus sensually satisfying himself, the chest's lid cracks his skull and his guests discover him brainless. The version in the *Libro de los exenplos por A.B.C. (Alphabetical Book of Apologues)* (ed. J. E. Keller, 1961, Chap. CXI), as well as others (Knust, pp. 336–37), are dull, sparkless reruns. Juan Manuel has, appropriately, a miser who is a Lombard from Bologna whose ill-gotten lucre causes his greedy sons to let him pass through his final agony without seeing the friar. Later in this weakly structured story, his heart is discovered, not in his body, but decaying and worm-ridden in his money chest. Lida de Malkiel has pointed out that Juan Manuel's attraction to the Dominicans incites him to utilize in his version the saint from Caleruega. St. Dominic is the only saint mentioned in *Count Lucanor.*

EXEMPLO 15. "Lorenzo Suárez at the Siege of Sevilla"

Here Don Juan Manuel draws on chronicled Castilian history, although incidents such as those involving the titled warrior Suárez Gallinato, modified by the author for use in tales 15 and

28, surely circulated orally in an age so fond of storytelling. The Count has asked what his stance should be in the face of rumored danger. Patronio relates how three foolhardy knights reacted when approached by a Moslem army, the moral being: Never act rashly, ignore rumors, play your strong hand only after it has been forced and after public opinion is on your side. Uprisings are caused often by rumormongering wretches who then plunder under cover of the turmoil. Patronio's lengthy commentary before and after the historical anecdote is a sign of Juan Manuel's interest in such a topic.

EXEMPLO 16. "The Reply of Fernán González"

Another anecdote from Castilian history has caught the author's attention: the story (*Poema de Fernán González,* stanza 346f) of how, during a moment of peace in Burgos, Fernán González is encouraged to give up the struggle of protecting his lands; he answers that there can be no quitting, since what is remembered after a man is dead is what he accomplished. Juan Manuel adds a splendidly descriptive line to the Castilian hero's reply in which the latter invites his weaker allies to fetch their best falcons, get on their fine fat mules, and spend their time hunting up and down the Arlanzón valley, if they are too soft for the good fight. Lida de Malkiel (*Estudios*, p. 106) believes that the adage appended by Don Juan to the anecdote, "The man died but his name lived on," was such an effective touch that it has influenced modern versions of this saying, in some of which a count (Fernán González) is mentioned. Don Juan's emphatic concern for the glory that trails a man's name, uncharacteristic of his age, is here again apparent, although Lida de Malkiel does not believe that he ever discourses abstractly on the notion of posthumous glory as such, but only in terms of a man's public reputation in the minds of his fellowmen, i.e., the Spanish *honra*.[18]

EXEMPLO 17. "An Insincere Invitation to Dine"

A brief, slight episode that asks a curious question: Should one accept something that he desperately wants when he knows that it is being offered only for courtesy's sake? The answer is affirmative, as a man, once rich but now starving, is halfheartedly invited to dine, knows that he is not expected to accept, yet proceeds to wash up and dive into the food. Don Juan seeks unsuccessfully to provide a humorous touch in the guest's acceptance speech. The meal somehow signals the return of good fortune: Don Juan is attracted by stories of well-to-do individuals who lose everything and later overcome their poverty. The *exemplo* is atypical since the author here throws out for consideration a problem of personal relationships and then manufactures an original scene to illustrate his solution.

EXEMPLO 18. "Pero Meléndez' Broken Leg"

The moral is Christian resignation before life's vicissitudes, since God's hand moves in mysterious ways, as witness this broken leg that prevented Meléndez from taking a trip on which he was to be murdered. Although Meléndez' cry: "My leg is broken, but God knows what's best!" is proverbial, it was other, older versions of similar proverbs (i.e., *Quod Deus fecit id bonum est*, Knust, p. 346) that generated this and other like *exempla* in Latin compilations. Menéndez Pelayo thought Meléndez a historical Adelantado of León, but the critic was deceived by Juan Manuel's fictional artistry in reclothing a timeless tale that is so old that it antedates the Talmudic compilations.[19]

EXEMPLO 19. "The Owls and the Crows"

Treachery is the theme of this Eastern tale, as a crow deludes the enemy into thinking him a friend. The retelling here is with a third-person directness that is typically Manueline, and without the excursus that drags out the version in *Calila e Digna* (ed. J. E. Keller and R. W. Linker, 1967, Ch. VI, p. 197f).

EXEMPLO 20. "The King and the False Alchemist"

This sprightly tale of deception, told earlier in the *Caballero Zifar* (ed. C. P. Wagner, 1929, p. 446f), is highlighted by its humor: a rascal deceives a gullible monarch into thinking that he has given him the alchemist's recipe for producing one gold *dobla*. One of the ingredients, however, is a metal ball that secretly contains, among other things, the dust of one *dobla*. A local dealer in overseas wares has been supplied with a hundred of these underpriced nuggets by the trickster, who blithely announces that they are a substance used by alchemists called *tabardíe*. *Tabardíe* is a meaningless, and therefore appropriately mysterious, word in the context of the tale; possible derivations from Arabic and Berber suggested by critics, meaning in these languages something worthless ("dirt, rags"), would, if plausible, add a new dimension to Juan Manuel's version and provide a delightfully ironic touch. Naturally the *tabardíe* is soon exhausted, and the sharpster offers to secure more in a distant land. The king supplies him with abundant wealth for the journey, and he is never seen again. A neat twist is provided at the end: Some townsfolk are playfully describing each citizen, and the king, qualified among those easily duped, says that their listing will prove incorrect should the voyager return. The list won't really change, they say, we'll simply put his name in place of yours.

EXEMPLO 21. "The Prince and His Tutor"

This lesson in modern pedagogy, with its medieval touches in the augur's use of birds as omens and the rending of garments to express grief, underscores the applied psychology necessary if the education of youth is to be successfully carried out.

EXEMPLO 22. "The Lion and the Bull"

Again, in a stretch of highly repetitious and verbose prose, Juan Manuel treats the theme of the destruction of private and public relationships and the inevitability of open conflict if the agents of discord are permitted to sow their seeds of fear.

EXEMPLO 23. "The Wise and Industrious Ants"

Some version of Pliny's explanation of the foresightedness of ants in first eating the germ in the grain to prevent its taking root when wet and demolishing their house is utilized in this practical lesson. In no place does Don Juan make any clearer his feelings toward living and dying *onrado,* i.e., having set before society the example expected and required of a man of his status.

EXEMPLO 24. "The Test of the Three Princes"

A sample of Juan Manuel at his storytelling best: the Eastern tale, well known in the West, of the king's choice of his youngest son to be king, is adapted to a Moslem setting attractive to Don Juan; the pace does not lag; there are touches of external reality (the Moslem garments, the Mosque) in this Moorish town; there is wry humor when the eldest son, having completed his inspection trip through town, to the accompaniment of an escort of royal musicians, announces that the town seemed fine but that he had a splitting headache from the blaring music. Patronio's preamble deals interestingly with medieval views on the relations between one's physical makeup and the psychology of one's character. The eternal discussion of the Spaniard's liver is not a modern theme; for Don Juan Manuel it is already an important topic.

EXEMPLO 25. "The Count of Provence"
This is the quasi-chivalresque tale of the young man who, chosen to be the husband of a Count's daughter for his personal qualities rather than his social status or his wealth, proves his mettle by rescuing his father-in-law after a series of mystifying moves that include deserting his bride as they prepare to bed down for the night, walking off with the entire family fortune, secretly acquiring and scattering a fleet of ships about every Armenian port, learning to speak Arabic (or Turkish), and becoming the house guest of the Count's captor, Saladin, a popular figure in medieval *exempla*. The lesson is that one's inner qualities (not inherited wealth or blood) are the only indicators of true manliness, and the motif is ancient and widespread. Both Lope in his *La pobreza estimada (Poverty Vindicated)* and Calderón in his *El Conde Lucanor* use Juan Manuel's prose romance as their immediate plot source.[20] Calderón curiously gives his protagonist the name Count Lucanor, and appears to think of him as a personality with traits he believed characteristic of Don Juan Manuel himself.

EXEMPLO 26. "The Tree of Falsehood"
This lesson encouraging truthfulness is illustrated with a parable of Truth and Falsehood personified. The visible portion of the tree of Falsehood is deceptively attractive, but Truth, initially relegated to its roots, by destroying them causes the downfall of Falsehood.

EXEMPLO 27. "The Emperor's Wife; the Wife of Alvar Fáñez Minaya"
In the first of this unit's two tales, the Emperor Fradrique asks the Pope to divorce him from his impossibly quarrelsome wife. The Pope refuses, but, aware of the nature of this woman,

adds that the Emperor's executive talents should enable him to handle the situation, and in any case, he, the Pope, could not consider the appropriate penance for a sin that had never taken place. While this blatant invitation has disturbed a few people,[21] what follows is even juicier: the coldly and casuistically planned disposal of the woman by telling her not to anoint her rash with a hellebore salve used to poison arrows. The contrary creature acts as expected, and is soon observed frothing and shaking in her final throes. Juan Manuel delicately has the Emperor away on a hunting trip when the woman is rattling about in her final agony. Women in the vanguard of liberating their sex will be delighted to know that the lesson in this *exemplo* is not what steps should be taken when divorce is impossible, but the importance of promptly and firmly breaking in a new wife to what is expected of her. The labels of cynic and materialist applied to Juan Manuel on the basis of *exemplos* such as this are exaggerated and out of tune with the fourteenth century. The core of the tale here is a hoary, traditional theme, and all that matters here is that the author thought it a good story. He used it for that reason.

The second tale is the story of a wife inanely virtuous and obedient; its painfully developed plot, however, in contrast to the previous story, likely made it as indigestible in the fourteenth century as it is in the twentieth. Don Juan Manuel's utilization of a fictionalized backdrop of Castilian history, populated with the figures of the Cid's nephew, Alvar Fáñez, and Pedro Ansúrez, represents, nevertheless, a creative advance in Castilian fiction.

EXEMPLO 28. "The Murderer of the Renegade Priest"

In another story built around anecdotal Castilian history from the days of his grandfather, Fernando III, Don Juan pictures in the flattering manner that is his wont a slice of Moslem Spain ruled by a tolerant caudillo. The Christian in exile so benevolently dealt with in Islamic territory is Lorenzo Suárez Gallinato, who, the chronicles tell us, was in real life a rebellious noble well received in Moslem-held Ecija. Don Juan freely embroiders the story line as he sees fit; the interwoven surface details provide a concreteness that casts over the whole plot an aura of historical truth. The protagonist is here imagined engaging in that one dramatic, death-defying act that is soul-saving reparation for a life of double treason, a situation immensely appealing to the author. Don Lorenzo, observing a mass said in mockery by the renegade for the amusement of a Moslem crowd, removes the priest's head with his sword and kneels before the mud-covered yet consecrated host.[22] While preparing to fight to a perfectly acceptable death at this point in his life, Suárez is rescued by the admiring Moslem king.

EXEMPLO 29. "The Fox Who Played Dead"

Don Juan Manuel's version of the popular Eastern tale of the fleeing fox who plays possum as passersby cut away parts of his anatomy for medicinal purposes (including warding off the evil eye), may be compared unfavorably with the lively strophes (1412–20) in Juan Ruiz's *Book of Good Love.*

EXEMPLO 30. "The Whims of Romayquia"

The moralizing here, on the theme of ingratitude, is of no interest whatever since it is simply a pretext for retelling these three anecdotes, simply an afterthought once the urge was upon Don Juan to narrate them. The intriguing aspect in this *exemplo,* as is the case in almost a fifth of them, is the author's utilization of material that apparently circulated as folklore among the Spanish Moslems on both sides of the frontier.[23] The three episodes deal with the childish demands of the beautiful wife of al-Mu'tamid, the eleventh-century Moslem sovereign-poet of Sevilla, whose tragic career itself enriched his people's lore. Juan Manuel is clearly delighted with the rich aroma of a Moslem royal court in Córdoba, whose exotic elements can scarcely be described; in one instance, Don Juan invites the reader to imagine how it must have been. Psychological characterizations of this stern symbol of Castilian orthodoxy might take into account the two scenes that he is amused to describe here: A mountain range is planted with almond trees so that their white February blossoms will satisfy a concubine's whim to see snow, and a great reservoir is flooded with perfumes and spices (a sumptuous listing is provided) in order to create a suitable place in which a barefoot woman might romp at her pleasure. Oh pale daughters of the Castilian steppes, listen to this tale of Córdoba and imagine how it must have been . . .

EXEMPLO 31. "The Franciscans in Paris"

A long, costly lawsuit between the Friars Minor, here apparently studying in Paris, and the regular cathedral priests over who would ring matins ends abruptly as a Cardinal, burning the mountains of testimony, determines that whoever gets up first can ring first. María Rosa Lida, finding a Dominican behind every bush, sees in this tale a humorous story with a Dominican point of view, since it chides their rivals, the Franciscans.

EXEMPLO 32. "The King's Clothes"

The story popularized today in H. C. Andersen's version is given a snappy ending as a black worker in the royal stables, whose social status is unaffected no matter who his father was, cuts through the sham and informs the king that he is parading around stark naked. It has been suggested that Cervantes' use of the motif of invisible material in his *Tableau of Miracles* was derived from this story. Don Juan's impatience with long-windedness, a marked feature of his approach to narrative, causes him to break off in midparagraph, bring his tale to a complete stop, and address the reader directly and rather briskly (*¿Qué vos diré más?*: "Haven't we been through this enough already?") in this and other (48, 50) *exemplos.*

EXEMPLO 33. "The Hawk and the Eagle"

Once considered original, but no longer so after the studies of Krappe and Lida de Malkiel,[24] this spirited story of the hawk who has the heart to fight off a larger aggressor and bring down his appointed prey is nevertheless a remarkable recasting of a traditional theme. Don Juan Manuel, aware that the bald tale itself will not suffice artistically, brings it to life with two simple, initial strokes that vitalize the setting: The reader now envisions the Toledan woods near Escalona, and the hawk rests on the arm of his father, the Infante Manuel. Such fictional touches have seduced more than one critic into believing this tale and others factual or even autobiographical. Patronio's admonishments here regarding the public responsibilities of a *grand señor* are powerful indications of the author's personal creed. When face to face with his God, a man of his station will have more than most to answer for. He must see that his life is lived purposefully, "it not being seemly that any *grand señor* should sit eating his bread, having done nothing to earn it." War against Islam can be expiation for a man's many sins, but only if he rides into the teeth of the enemy with an honest conscience; the fatal step is to delude oneself. This proviso is crucial, as elsewhere he mocks those hypocrites who seek salvation by rushing off to die in battle. The author cross-references the third *exemplo* here, indicating his view of the *Lucanor* as a unified whole.

EXEMPLO 34. "When One Blind Man Leads Another"
The Count's opening question and Patronio's closing caveat deal with the former's fear of lodging in a certain town or castle to which he has been urged to ride by a friend or relative. The tale is a meager gloss of the widely popularized parable deriving initially from Matthew XV: 14 and Luke VI: 39.

EXEMPLO 35. "The Youth and His Ferocious Bride"
As the tale that is unfailingly selected for most American anthologies and school readers, this *exemplo* is the first item recalled by the student at the mention of Don Juan Manuel. It is not immediately clear why in the twentieth century this should have been the most popularized of the fifty-four *exemplos*, although the story, using the same theme found later in Shakespeare's *Taming of the Shrew*, is admittedly well put together here. The tale's origins lie remotely in Eastern fiction and as a stock anecdote it is well known in Western folklore. Juan Manuel's version is marked with a sprightly use of dialogue. Local color is provided by references to Moslem wedding practices, and the twist at the end, as the old husband tries to emulate the firm hand of the youth, provides a humorous turnabout that is the right touch to top off the tale's amusing tone.

EXEMPLO 36. "The Merchant Who Found His Wife and Son in Bed"
This is the story, long known in the West, of the husband who returns home after a long absence and suspects the worst upon finding his wife in the company of his unrecognized son, who in Don Juan's version is a youth older than twenty. This interesting situation has attracted the attention of Valbuena Prat, a critic Freudian overtones do not escape easily.[25] Don Juan has the youth in his mother's bed, where he has spent his nights inno-

cently since birth, and where, while providing a kind of mock security for the poor woman in her desperate longing for the boy's father, he is called "husband" by his emotionally distressed mother; the latter, after a twenty-year wait for word from her husband, would appear to have a perfect right to be emotionally distressed. In this and other versions, an unfortunate but necessary point in the narrative is the wife's need to remind her husband that she was pregnant when he left. In one version the son is still a baby, and the husband, approaching in the dark, only hears two people in the bed. Those who would make of this tale a curiosity of some kind are deluding themselves. Juan Manuel simply wants to tell a better story. He wants to portray an older husband shaken with murderous rage at the sight of his wife dining and sleeping with a much younger, strapping youth, and a woman so distraught she must either fabricate her own private dreamworld or face mental disintegration.

The popular topos of the teacher-philosopher (*grand maestro*) who has for sale wise sayings at reasonable prices is the frame within the frame of *exemplo 36*. Don Juan writes with a fine mild irony here. Before his first purchase, the merchant views the transaction with a suspicion proper to his profession, and for his carefully spent penny he is told: When one is invited out to dine and does not know what the meal will consist of, it is best to load up heavily on the first course served. Hearing this sparkling gem of advice, the merchant sputters doubt that he has received his money's worth, but the philosopher, who knows something of economics himself (he always has the coin in hand before the wisdom flows from his mouth), replies that it was a bargain, considering the price. Sensing that he is throwing good money after bad, but caught up in a game of bargaining that he should be familiar with, the merchant then asks for a dollar's worth. He is told: Never let a violent rage sweep you into some senseless act; always calmly gather all the facts first. The merchant surmises that the going rate will soon empty his purse with no return, but, being a good businessman, he stores in his heart this second bit of wisdom. It is to be a substantial bargain, since it prevents two senseless murders. In the fourteenth century, carrying on a strong tradition of wisdom literature, it is wise to believe in wise sayings.

EXEMPLO 37. "The Reply of Fernán González"

A backdrop of Castilian history is again used, this time to eulogize dedication to duty in difficult times. Chronicles and poetry before and during Don Juan's lifetime tell of a war-weary Fernán González whose army suffers terrible losses in the tenth-century victory over the Moslem caudillo Almanzor at Hacinas, near Salas. Although it has been stated that Don Juan here creates a totally fictitious account, this is not entirely the case. It is obvious that he has read the *Poem of Fernán González* and was impressed by the warrior's splendid calls of encouragement to his men and by the severe wounds sustained by the Castilians in the bloody encounter at Hacinas. He doubtless also noted the Castilians' fear (stanzas 434–35) of the reactions of their unfriendly neighbors, the Navarrese. Don Juan then rewrote the incident, incorporating all these elements as he saw fit, and capping it with an invasion of Castile by Navarrese troops. When the Castilians cry to their leader that their broken bodies must now rest, Don Juan has the classic father-figure of Castilian history tell his men that their old wounds will be of no concern once they begin acquiring new wounds. Juan Manuel has thus deftly created an anecdote with which to admonish lazy Castilian youth, since the line separating historical truth from fictional anecdote only requires a short time to disappear. It is stressed here that much more than Fernán González' life and property are at stake; a man's *onra,* with all that the Spanish word implies, may hang in the balance.

EXEMPLO 38. "The Man Who Drowned with His Riches"

The tale here is of the gem-laden traveler who so values his cargo that he is blind to the fact that he is about to lose much more than the gems. He sinks gradually out of sight in the river channel, clutching his precious burden. The moral is obvious, but while belaboring it, Patronio's lesson neatly capsules what will be accepted convention in the Golden Age's literary code of honor: "What a man thinks of himself has no bearing on his reputation; his name stands out only to the extent that his actions cause others to think highly of him."

EXEMPLO 39. "The Sick Man and the Noisy Birds"

Forced to choose between ridding himself of either the louder but often absent swallows or the quieter but always present sparrows, a sickly insomniac decides to banish the latter. The lesson indicated here, in a quickly dispatched message, is that it is preferable to attack an enemy close to one's home, even though more powerful opponents live elsewhere. This abbreviated *exemplo* may have been the last of several dictated by Don Juan on a very cold Castilian winter evening, shortly before retiring for the night.

EXEMPLO 40. "The Seneschal of Carcassonne"

Don Juan Manuel is often concerned with the double immortality of both soul and flesh, since the latter can have, in a man's name and what is said about that name, a lasting presence in the secular world, just as the former seeks its permanent destiny in the divine. In this tale of the wealthy steward who is condemned to hell for doing the right thing at the wrong time is revealed the author's preoccupation with interpreting the nuances of an authoritarian religious approach to the problems of salvation. He does not fail to point out, and this is indicative of his turn of mind, that the seneschal's underlying motives in writing a will that would donate sums after his death for good works on behalf of his soul are double: to insure his soul's salvation with funds not available to him (Don Juan uses the phrase: "You can't take it with you"), and to have the world remember him forever for his splendid generosity. Juan Manuel, forever fretting over the weight and meaning a man's name can acquire, has thought long about what must be avoided, as well as what is necessary, to achieve a kind of glory on earth.

This is a tale never mentioned when Don Juan's utilization of Dominican sources is discussed, since the goats here are the Dominicans, as well as the Franciscans, who announce vehemently that the sick man, confessed and anointed, is surely in heaven, even as he burns in hell. The woman possessed of the devil who so convincingly annihilates the friars' contention is an interesting feature: the author has his friars here humbly (and naturally) seek out a mad woman, in hopes of a vision of the world beyond the grave. This crazed female is a vehicle for the theological argument that what is in a man's mind outweighs his overt actions. It is never to one's advantage, according to the proverb used here by Don Juan, to steal a sheep and then, for the love of God, give away its feet to charity.

Little has been written about possible sources for this thinly constructed, one-page narrative. It would appear that there are few sources that can be posited in the customary fashion, although vaguely parallel examples of this or that motif can naturally always be conjectured. Juan Manuel wants to write about a topic often in his thoughts, and he simply goes about making his point. The external touches, of course, all have their individual sources in the author's experience, but what is important is that they are brought together here to achieve a narrative impact in typical juanmanuelistic fashion: a site in southern France, distant enough to be somewhat exotic, yet so recognizable that merely concretizing the action there provides an aura of credibility; a steward who is the perfect choice, a quasi-biblical shadow of a figure who unwisely sets about managing affairs of the spirit in much the same fashion that he doubtless employed for material matters; a demonic female who wanders into town one day with the devil in her brain, spouting truths so extraordinary that friars pause to look at each other questioningly. Very few in the audience will want to remain to hear a sermon on the proper conduct of almsgiving, which is what is being preached in *exemplo 40;* none will leave, however, as long as there is a mad woman loose within the great wall of Carcassonne.

EXEMPLO 41. "Al-Hakam Caliph of Córdoba"

Here Don Juan is again attracted to an anecdote, originating in the Moslem world to the south and circulating in Christian territory, that culminates in an Arabic proverb.[26] The story of al-Hakam II, the tenth-century caliph famed for his learning and his library of four hundred thousand volumes, is sketched in a well-rounded, capsule-like tale: Here pleasure-loving and lazy, and criticized by his people for his inactivity, he is pictured relaxing pleasantly one day in a scene deftly set by the author, when it occurs to him that the quality of the flute music serenading his senses might be improved by cutting another hole in the instrument. The addition results in a better tone, and word of this minor invention moves the people to create a proverb repeated whenever they wished to belittle with sarcasm someone's accomplishment: "This is like the famous creation of al-

Hakam," "This is what al-Hakam accomplished," they would say. He despairs of his reputation after forcing his embarrassed attendants to reveal the origin of the saying, but then, in an effort to secure a worthy place in history, he supervises the expansion and elaboration of the great Mosque of Córdoba, "the noblest in all of Moslem Spain." Thereafter, his splendid task completed, the man's reputation brought on an event that must have been sheer delight for fame-conscious Don Juan Manuel to savor and relate: The very meaning of the proverb changed to indicate sincere praise for any task well done. Discussion has centered indecisively on the amount of original detail that Don Juan has added to the story, but it appears likely that, starting with the proverb and its historical references, he constructed the basic fabric of the tale out of his imagination, endowing it with that aura of reality that is his special talent.

Exemplo 41 is distinctive for the unusual nature of its frame. The Count is concerned because his friends are mocking him (in good-natured jesting presumably, but the text gives the opposite impression) by adding to a list of the stalwart giants of Castilian history (the Cid, Fernán González, San Fernando) and their enormous feats, the name of the Count himself and his "glorious" accomplishment: He has made minor improvements in the leather devices used in falconry to hood the bird and band its legs. Contrary to its basically objective character, the frame here appears to bear the very personal imprint of Juan Manuel himself. The Count brags of his hunting prowess, much as Don Juan was wont to do, and then laments that he is scorned for worthwhile contributions to the sport, which may seem insignificant to some, but are certainly no cause for his being made the butt of their jokes. Some may be tempted to see behind these lines a petulant and short-tempered Juan Manuel overreacting to rumors of things said about him, or even misinterpreting remarks reaching him secondhand, but the point that he is making in this *exemplo,* that one must live a public life that places himself above all trifling criticism, overrides such contentions.

EXEMPLO 42. "The Pious Hypocrite and Her Lies"

This apologue on the disastrous effect of a slandering tongue is a story retold many times, and one which Don Juan unfortunately does not noticeably improve in his version.[27] The devil, contriving to bring discord to a happily married couple, uses the services of an old woman called a *beguina* who, by planting seeds of mistrust in the couple's thoughts, sees her insinuations bear fruit in a relentless series of brutal murders. Beguines were (and still are) members of a semireligious congregation of lay women, founded in Belgium in the twelfth century, that spread rapidly over most of Europe before its condemnation by John XXII in 1311. Its attractiveness both to orthodox believers and to others preaching individual forms of Christianity continued, nevertheless, well into the low Middle Ages, and they (a male branch had been added) may be found, then, still listed in orthodox Corpus processions with Franciscans, Dominicans, etc. The stigma of heresy had gone unrelieved from the very first, however, and the word *beguina* appears in Juan Manuel's text to mean primarily someone who deceptively pretends to be something she is not. Lida de Malkiel has pointed out the frequency with which *beguinas* were the objects of the Dominicans' ire; she wonders, since in the older versions quoted by Knust the protagonist is usually simply called *vetula* (old woman), whether Don Juan is here influenced by his Dominican sources or is expressing his own distaste for unorthodox religious groups. Don Juan uses *beguinería* in the *Unfinished Book* as a synonym for "hypocrisy."

EXEMPLO 43. "The Story of Good and Evil; the Wise Man and the Fool"

The first of the two tales in *exemplo 43* is an abbreviated morality play in which Good and Evil divide the benefits from five communal properties. Evil maliciously, or naturally, takes advantage of Good's good-natured ways and attaches for himself the most profitable products in each case: from the ewes, Evil takes the wool and milk, without which Good's lambs soon perish; from the swine, the offspring, with Good the recipient of the swine's wool and milk; from the turnip crop, the roots, as Good is apportioned the greens; from the cabbages, the greens, with the roots reverting to Good. Their fifth jointly-owned property is a woman, and the best part of her is the part from the waist down. Good's half of the woman, from the waist up, does the housework for him during the day, and the other half performs for its owner during the night. When a child is born and cries for milk, it becomes immediately clear to all parties that none is to be obtained from the waist down. With this leverage the balance of power now swings to Good, who feeds the child and forces Evil to confess in a public parade through town that his malicious ways are conquered by kindness. The abstract figures are occasionally not so abstract, but are rather finely characterized as the author feels the urge to enliven the story's movement: When Evil discovers to his horror that Good has denied the child the milk, he approaches Good wearing his best crow-eating grin, but his laughter and jokes at this moment reveal his awareness that this is no matter for laughter and joking.

The second tale here is another of the several in which the story line builds into a folk proverb. This is the story, well known in Juan Manuel's day, of the village idiot whose idea of fun on a dull afternoon is to bounce rocks and buckets off the naked customers hopping around helplessly in the local public bath. The decline in business at this establishment soon reaches alarming proportions, when early one day the owner himself, naked and armed with boiling water and a club, charges from his hiding place in the bath and violently lays into the village fool. The latter runs screaming into the street, announcing that "there is another loco in the bathhouse."

Don Juan has had to stretch his imagination somewhat to devise a suitable introduction once the decision was made to use these stories. Count Lucanor's problem here is how to react to mistreatment from people with whom one has either close ties or no ties at all. The adviser's solution is to strike back in the latter case, but make every effort to overlook flaws in the case of one's friends.

EXEMPLO 44. "The Loyal Men of Don Rodrigo el Franco"

This tale of extraordinary devotion and loyalty appeals to few readers today, but Don Juan may be here very near the peak of his storytelling art. Utilizing historical figures from twelfth-century Castile and anecdotes wherever he has picked them up, he gives himself free rein to overdramatize whenever his intuition tells him that audiences enjoy being overwhelmed and occasionally shocked. This quasi-romance, beginning with a man finding his body covered at once with leper sores and ending with a woman plunging a needle into her eye, also has an occasional stomach-wrenching scene along the way, as it runs a course designed to keep the audience awake. The second wife accused of adultery, literally on her way to be burned at the stake, curiously admits that, although she did not sleep with the man, she really wanted to. This remarkable display of candor momentarily bewilders the man offering to fight for her in a trial by combat. He decides that even if God adjudges the ordeal in the woman's favor and he wins in the field, there will be a penalty of some kind. There is: He loses an eye. The author's picture of the bedraggled heroes, so wretched and almost unrecognizable in their rags, yet returning in glory to Castile, adds a touch purely romantic in its audience appeal.

EXEMPLO 45. "The Man Who Made a Pact with the Devil"

This version of an unusually popular story is similar to that found in the *Book of Good Love*. It serves here as an attack on the flourishing business done by sorcerers who use magic circles and the like to call upon the services of the Devil. The author has Patronio name two figures, prominent in fourteenth-century Castilian politics and well known to Don Juan, who were both addicted to the reading of omens and met violent ends. The mention of their deaths aids in determining the beginning of the composition of this work. Garcilaso de la Vega and Alvar Núñez Osorio had been intimate advisers of the fifteen-year-old Alfonso XI in 1325. The former was murdered while hearing mass in Soria; Núñez Osorio, Count of Trastámara, was assassinated on orders of Alfonso XI in 1328.

EXEMPLO 46. "The Wise Man and the Prostitutes"

A reasonable assumption here is that the gist of this tale, of unidentified origin and with a Moroccan setting, is from some Arabic source, although this plainly never means that Don Juan necessarily extracted it from that source firsthand. A major part of the text, both story and frame, is devoted to a discussion of the vicissitudes that affect a man's reputation among his peers, a subject to which Don Juan constantly returns. The relations between his ideas here and the literary themes of Benign and Adverse Fortune, and of Honor/Vengeance, in later centuries, is a topic that could be taken up at some length. The story itself is unimpressive and does not really interest Don Juan; he is eager to elucidate the moral point of this unit. The tale's treatment of the philosopher's lower intestinal tract and of his sojourn in a red-light district is well within the range and scope of incidents in *exemplum* literature.

In the narrative, a loved and respected old philosopher, having apparently spent a lifetime of inactivity with his books, has become one of the really slow movers of his age. His doctors have warned him that in the future, whenever nature calls, he must not postpone his response, or his health, already poor, will be more seriously impaired. Then, as will happen to even the best of men, he is on his way through town one day to meet his students, when an urgent and unmistakable signal sends him into a side street, where, unknown to him, the local prostitutes are all in business. After a long and strenuous hour in the alley that has nothing at all to do with the area's principal commercial activity, the aged professor makes his way rather weakly back onto the main thoroughfare; he does not appear to be in very good shape. Thus observed, he soon discovers his reputation ruined by the spreading gossip, and the story ends abruptly as he composes an essay for his pupils on the slender thread that holds a man's reputation. Major points stressed by Don Juan are that the philosopher's respected position in society, earned during a lifetime of dedicated service, made him a prime subject for malicious gossip, because people are such that they prefer to hear bad things about good people; that what mattered was who he was, not what they thought he did; and the helplessness of the individual and the irrevocable public destruction of his name, once the scandalmongers eagerly plied their vicious trade.

EXEMPLO 47. "The Moslem Girl Easily Scared"

More than one commentator believes that Juan Manuel is here inventing an imaginary background to a Moslem proverb. If this is not the case, it is still certainly clear that the story and its detailed elaboration, and not the weakly phrased pretext and moral that accompany it, are his only concern here; he simply wants to tell this story, and does so with rich detail. An impoverished Moslem youth survives by robbing recently filled graves of the fineries buried with the corpses. He supports a pampered sister who is treated with deference since she has convincingly conveyed the idea that she is frightened by everything, even the glug-glug sound of the liquid drunk from long-necked Moorish jars.[28] Upon learning that an unusually rich grave is to be violated one night, however, she accompanies her brother only to discover that the valuable garments cannot be removed intact from the cadaver unless the dead man's head is wrenched to the point of dislocating his neck. Without giving it a second thought, she proceeds to accomplish this with her own delicate little hands. The realization dawns on her brother that, for his sister, the only real difference between the glug-glug of the water and the crunch-crunch of the bones was what she was accomplishing for herself. His comment in Arabic on her two-faced nature, transcribed and translated by Don Juan, has become, he says, a popular saying among Moslems.

EXEMPLO 48. "The Half Friend and the Whole Friend"

With so universal a theme as the definition of true friendship, it is not difficult to understand the popularity of this age-old tale that was apparently circulating in its several versions in the eastern Mediterranean even before Muhammad became prophet. In the West the high note usually occurs when "friends" are asked to hide a blood-stained sack believed to contain a corpse; the true friend's willingness to do so is used by the father (or old man) to illustrate the fact that most of one's so-called friends are of the fair-weather variety. The final events in Juan Manuel's version are due to his decision at the outset that the action of the "whole friend" would necessarily involve the giving of a life for a friend, thus providing an easy transition into a discourse on Christ's sacrifice on the cross.[29]

EXEMPLO 49. "The Man Left Naked on an Island"

The primary theme here derives from the abundantly popular Eastern story of the man (or any man) who is allowed to act as king for a set period of time, a motif employed in Calderón's *Life is a Dream.* Don Juan's utilization is quite simple: He adapts it to the Christian ethic of living this life in such a way as to find happiness in the next. Man finishes this secular journey as stripped of worldly goods as are this tale's rulers, doomed to be cast away naked on an island.

EXEMPLO 50. "Saladin and His Vassal's Wife"

This, the longest *exemplo* of all, is occasionally labeled, when infelicitous comparisons are made between Don Juan Manuel and Boccaccio, as the only one with a theme of sexual lust. Such a bald, unclarified comment is unfortunate; it is also a misleading characterization of a unit of this work that contains, in Patronio's interpretive preaching, a rounded picture of Juan Manuel's views that provides insights into the *Lucanor* as a whole and the author's reasons for writing it.[30] Here it becomes plain for the modern reader that Don Juan's insistence on the necessity of improving one's position materially, seen in the many *exemplos* that project attitudes on the surface selfish and self-serving, is not incompatible with his overall vision of what a Castilian nobleman like himself must do to save his soul. Obviously a man may seek wealth for the wrong reasons; Don Juan would think the reader stupid who did not understand that a priori. A noble born to landed possessions in fourteenth-century Castile did not ask to be so born; his status in a divinely ordered society is served by improving his holdings. The crux of the problem is that he do so for the right reasons and without breaking God's law.

Thus the lengthy story of Saladin concentrates on the single gut issue: What is the most important, the most crucial, quality a man's character can have? The answer, in view of the confusing nature of life itself and the difficult decisions faced constantly, is that a man must have a conscience. The man has not lived who has not sinned, but there is hope for any man whose actions are guided ultimately by his conscience. Such a man will accomplish the "good works" necessary in this life if his soul is to be redeemed, works that benefit himself (and thereby, naturally, the segment of society he is responsible to and for) and his God. No ordering of priorities is intended in this phrasing; none exists. This is a theme at the heart of Don Juan Manuel's thinking.

The narrative itself displays a medieval fondness for posing riddles and abstract or philosophical problems, after which the wise men are called in to quarrel over the answers. The woman (her husband having been sent away, as in the story of Uriah) has promised to accede to the Sultan's desires if he tells her the most beneficial quality a man's character can have. The story of his long search for the answer offers several interesting episodes,

including one in which the monarch disguises himself as a jongleur in order to travel about with two other minstrels, and another in which the vassal's wife complains of the sexual abuse
of women, particularly by the nobility of her day. At the tale's
conclusion, in which the woman's honor is left intact, Patronio
recalls that he has answered fifty questions and desires a respite
after one more. He mentions curiously that many of the Count's
friends are upset because he has spent so much time on this
project.

EXEMPLO 51. "The King Guilty of Pride"
    The language and tone of this story are cause for considering
it a part of the original work, despite the hesitation felt by some
at the asymmetry of the numbering (even though 51 is divisible
by 3). The author has decided earlier that an appropriate ending
to his book will be this story on the sin of sins and the root of
man's descent into wickedness, and Patronio has already announced this final tale. The theme of the mighty who are cast
down was well known in Western lore, and here Don Juan re-
tells the Robert of Sicily story of the arrogant monarch, found
also in the *Gesta Romanorum,* who lives a wretched beggar's life
when his bodily form on the throne is assumed by an angel.[31]
The lesson in humility that he learns, as is often the case in the
medieval scheme of virtues, is incarnate in the figure of the simple, unassuming Jewish maiden whose stunned mind knows only
humility at the news that she is to bear the Son of God. It would
be difficult to overassess the impact of this manner of depicting
Mary on medieval Christianity, and there is no problem in
recognizing Juan Manuel's strongly felt devotion to the Virgin,
expressed throughout his works. But his concern here is especially directed at the outward signs of humility displayed by
some who inwardly have no such feelings, and Patronio abruptly
breaks off his narration at one point to criticize these hypocrites.

IV *The Four Added Sections*
    After the fifty-one units of the *Lucanor* were written, the book
ostensibly finished and copies of it possibly even read by the
author's friends, Don Juan made his decision to add four extra
chapters.[32] He appears to do so most unwillingly. He explains his
action, in a brief introductory passage in the first of his appended

chapters, by pleading that his good friend Jaime, a baron from Jérica, has asked him to write in an *oscuro* style, i.e., a manner not so plain and simple, more profound in its elaboration than, say, his usual straightforward technique. (Jérica, today politically in Castellón, was integrally at that time, of course, part of the Aragonese Kingdom, not very distant from either Don Juan's lands in the Alicante area, or his strongholds in southern Cuenca; its Aragonese master is esteemed by Juan as perhaps his best friend, doubtless because of his loyalty on occasions when armed clashes seemed inevitable.) It is always assumed that Don Juan understood exactly what his friend Jaime was requesting, and that what we have here, in these first three added sections that present bald lists of proverbs without commentary or elaboration (the fourth section is an essay with running text), is the sort of thing that Jaime actually had in mind when he asked for more "obscurity." This may or may not have been the case. It has even been suggested that Jaime must have been a snobbish or pedantic sort to request this kind of composition.

The first thought that occurs to Don Juan in this appendix comprising some of the most mind-dulling pages that he wrote is that it is much easier to write in a deep, obfuscating manner about subjects that are deep and obfuscating. Unfortunately, he says, he is not equipped to take up theology, philosophy, or the natural sciences; he will continue, therefore, to deal with his original theme, i.e., the day-to-day conduct of one's life and personal relationships that best provides for happiness both here and in the afterlife. His problem, then, is to make what he says *oscuro:* in other words, to do something that he abhors.

And so, his painful apprehension almost visually sensed by the reader, Juan Manuel proceeds to compose a lengthy series of aphorisms in three of the four appended chapters. He begins in the first chapter with a hundred proverbs, almost all learned, with only a rare item classifiable as folk: "Birds of a feather flock together." The bulk are such as, "Many use God's name but few walk His path," "A wise man can put up with a fool but the reverse is never true," "Ugly indeed is it to fast with one's mouth and sin with the rest of the body," "A man with real knowledge knows where his knowledge is deficient, while dolts always think that they know everything." In an occasional proverb in this first chapter, the author plays with words and their meanings, adding, in his opinion, "obscurity": *El rey rey, reyna; el rey non rey, non reyna, mas es reynado.* Such techniques are naturally of interest to students of Juan Manuel. This trend is increasingly evident in the second appended chapter, and in the third the author is seized with a mind-boggling inspiration that some have called puerile: He decides to add to his proverbs' difficulty by jumbling their normal word order. Thus they constitute puzzles of a quality somewhat less appealing than that found in Sunday Supplements, and while María Goyri and Sánchez Cantón have attempted to order them correctly, some have yet to be clearly deciphered.[33] It has been suggested that Don Juan is playing a joke here on his more erudite contemporaries, but such a theory is unacceptable.

For Don Juan Manuel, then, *oscuro,* practically synonymous here with *sotil,* simply describes a manner of writing succinct, erudite *sententiae* that requires the reader to make some effort to penetrate the first bare notion proffered by the words and grasp the profound truth that they ultimately project; the exercise is presumably thought provoking and has some pedagogical value. The student familiar with Old Spanish literature will at once see resemblances to the gnomic verse of Rabbi Sem Tob, as well as to the collections of learned aphorisms produced in the thirteenth century, especially prior to the flow of apologue collections from the middle of that century on.[34] It is customary in manuals to link Don Juan Manuel's brief moment at the shrine of obscurity to earlier and later cultivations of this genre, and especially to its pronounced worship in the Golden Age, but there is not here a similarity of evolving artistic attitudes that is easily discerned and digested, except perhaps in a most superficial way. When he concludes the three units of *sententiae,* it is with a sigh of relief that he turns to composing the final section of running expository prose on the themes of faith and salvation. A weary Patronio pleads for an end to the book.

It has been noted that the fourth and final appended section, a catechism and discussion-exposition of doctrinal matters, rounds out the author's presentation in this one book of examples of the three established didactic genres given currency in the preceding century: *exemplum*-collection; learned, pithy sayings; preceptive, doctrinal prose.[35] In the last-named Don Juan takes up the nature of religious faith; certain articles of belief, especially the

Eucharist and Baptism; and the problems in attaining salvation through good works, including particularly the touchy issue of making a distinction between an act and the intent in the mind of the person prior to the deed. The author more than once is disturbed that men of his social status must continually act precipitously and even violently, and may do so in good faith, only to discover later that the resultant situation has perverted their intentions. To drive home his point in this regard, he even incorporates in its entirety the tale of the son who kills his father in the tragic circumstance of their having to go to war for different masters. The arguments throughout are ordered scholastically and symmetrically under headings and subheadings, point by point, and they indicate Don Juan's familiarity with the formal style of theologian and philosopher.

This last essay is a rich, unmined lode for the study of the author's world picture: the medieval notion of "elements," the Thomistic principle of constant motion and generated change in a theocentric universe, the *natura*, in the medieval sense, of entities and events that present individually a self-contained and systematic inner logic that is clearly discernible to the inquisitive medieval scientific mind: the menstrual cycle, the sex act, the womb, the phenomena of seven-, eight-, nine-, and ten-month births, circumcision, and the like. Juan Manuel the etymologist is present, here as elsewhere, deriving the "original" of Original Sin from the child's "origins" at birth, stained with his parent's spasm of pleasure at conception, and tracing *mundo*, often meaning "universe" in the medieval language, to the etyma "motion" and "regeneration." Although Don Juan insists that the presentation of dogma be made *por razón*, i.e., scholastically, so that its validity is self-evident to pagan, heretic, Jew, and Moslem alike, as well as to Christians, he determines that at the critical moment of truth, in the face of eternity, a man's faith must be wholly and unquestioningly given, and the image drawn is not an unmoving one: He must believe as does that little old woman who sits quietly in her country doorway, spinning her thread in the sun.

Finally, it may be pointed out that although these appendices are edited at times as the Second, Third, etc., Parts of *Count Lucanor*, they were for the author an appended "book," which, despite the fact that it constituted a continuation of his original plan, begins with a "first part" and ends with a "fourth." The frame of mutually flattering dialogue between the importuning Count and his persevering adviser persists to the very end, with an occasional and customary third-person reference by the author to Don Johan, i.e., to himself.

V *The First Writer of Castilian Prose with an Individual, Personal Style*

The assessment in the words above by Menéndez Pelayo at the turn of the century is the one found repeatedly in manuals, and it is a valid one. Don Juan Manuel's contribution to the art of fiction is one that scarcely needs to be exaggerated. The aspects of style that concern him, his brevity, his emphatic preference for a vocabulary that is *castizo* or pure and thoroughly Castilian, the concrete detail of setting, the pace of the story, the touch of humor, the abrupt about-face in the story line, a not infrequent ironic smile, occasional crisp dialogue, absolute clarity to go with his conciseness, composition that is deliberate and carefully planned, an awareness of dramatic possibilities, all these need no further belaboring at this point. His primary contribution to the narrative art, however, goes beyond this. It occurs at those moments in *Count Lucanor* when the awareness that he is moralizing via the bare outline of an apologue slips away, and the creative urge is felt to polish and enliven the scene with a stroke of vivid detail, and to structure the telling so that one is drawn along out of sheer curiosity to the final, and perhaps unsuspected, turn of events. It is his awareness of himself as a writer, and as such, of his duty and desire to fulfill an artistic function, freely chosen, by molding the finished product into a form as aesthetically satisfying as his talents permit. His decision to utilize themes from Castilian history and his deft ability at turning a historical backdrop into fiction with a concrete detail or two, must especially not be underestimated. A new view of fiction is emerging, and Don Juan Manuel is its most obvious proponent.

The customary list of "themes" that are supposed to categorize the moral counsel in the *exemplos* is not included here; at times they were mentioned in the course of the individual discussions. To state baldly that certain of them deal with "honor" while others take up "friendship," etc., can be misleading if such abstract categorizing is not further substantially qualified. It is stated occasionally that the lessons in *Count Lucanor* make up a guidebook for living that is as valid today as it was in the fourteenth century. Such is certainly not the case. One can always extract a few superficial items of mundane counsel and call them a practical guide to life, but the advice in *Count Lucanor* is often meaningless if it is not interpreted in terms of the individual who wrote it and the goals of his stratum of society.

Frequent criticisms of his style concern his abundant use of conjunctions, resulting at times in seemingly endless, run-on sentences, and his avoidance of metaphors and rhetorical devices. While contributing to a certain rare bit of repetitiveness that is distracting to the modern reader, the former technique does not detract from the author's carefully pursued goal of clarity of thought and expression. Although it is generally noted that his language is a polished version of the basic vehicle of Alfonso X, the syntax of Juan Manuel in fact displays a far richer degree of subordination that provides a smoother, more fluid text. His lexical richness and variety are likewise substantially greater than that of his learned uncle.

Count Lucanor, in great contrast to other well-known works in medieval Castilian, has generally always enjoyed a continuing existence in print. The Jesuit philosopher Gracián in the Golden Age had the Argote de Molina edition at hand, as did the dramatists and others who helped themselves to the materials prepared by Juan Manuel. Even in the late Middle Ages the number of manuscripts may have been considerable; Giménez Soler states (p. 676) that a fifteenth-century letter to Ferrán López de Stúñiga asks that he forward a copy of that book called *El Conde Lucanor.*

CHAPTER 5

The Orthodox World of Don Juan Manuel

THE indelible mark of the author's personality is a clearly visible thread running through most of what Juan Manuel writes, and there is considerable truth in the repeated remark that what he really writes about most of the time is Don Juan Manuel. While the three works reserved for Chapter 6 (*Hunting, Assumption, Coat of Arms*) are often intensely personal documents, it will be clear also at every moment in the present chapter that those now considered are likewise indelibly and subjectively stamped. The books briefly described here (*Knight and Apprentice, Plan of Society, Unfinished Book*), and primarily the second of these, constitute a major portion of the author's writings that present the external world of fourteenth-century Castile seen through the eyes, mind, and conscience of Don Juan Manuel. They stand apart generally among his extant works through a likeness in the arrangement and presentation of information. The pedagogic element is stronger here than elsewhere, and in all three an older, wiser man is instructing a youth of noble background. There are substantial differences, however, especially in the *Unfinished Book:* The latter work, chronologically the last of the three, is without the fictional features found in the earlier works and its language appears to flow more smoothly. No study, unfortunately, has been done to determine evolving stylistic patterns throughout these works. In all three works the ever-present theme, never far from the surface of his discourse, and usually at the heart of whatever he is saying, is his preoccupation with a clear expression of what constitutes ethical conduct in the eyes of man and God.

I   Libro del cavallero et del escudero
(Book about the Knight and the Apprentice-Kinght)

In Chapters 90–91 of Juan Manuel's *Estados,* the wandering preacher Julio advises his pupil Joas that he may examine with profit the two splendid books on the chivalric code written by his former pupil, who in this fictional frame is none other than a Don Johan from the distant land of Castile: "One is called the *Book on Chivalry* and the other is the *Book of the Knight and the Apprentice*." Thus, as he often is fond of doing, Juan Manuel inserts himself and references to his former works into the didactic stream of later books, and what follows then in *Estados* is a lengthy, detailed table of contents that coincides closely with the moralizing and edifying passages of many chapters (especially 16–21, 31–50) in *Knight,* provided one deletes from the latter work the fictional narrative thread (the *fabliella*) and all discussions of natural history, and natural and supernatural phenomena, in their entirety. It would appear first, then, that the two works, one (*Chivalry*) lost, and the other (*Knight*), which will now be summarized, were closely related books in the author's mind, and that they were composed in the order in which their author lists them. But Don Juan himself (*Estados*, I, 90) adds a proviso with respect to the latter book, important in his mind at least, which is that "even though Don Johan composed this latter work utilizing the frame of a *fabliella*, it is (despite this) a book from which one may learn many things." The *fabliella* is the sugarcoating: It has a plot which could thicken but never does; it tells of interesting people who somehow never do interesting things; but if the reader's sweet tooth takes over, he will swallow the beneficial marrow as well as the sweetened veneer. And it is also quite convenient, since one now has a way of tying a series of short sermons together in an attractive package; they somehow seem less like sermons. It is possible that *Knight* is a work presenting much (but not exactly) the same expository detail on chivalric ritual and knightly behavior that was originally covered in *Chivalry,* but which encompasses it in a thin tale involving an old warrior and a youthful neophyte; it also apparently adds new material on spiritual matters and the external, material world for which the author had later found inspiration as he satisfied his appetite to discover and read new texts. A brief account of its contents follows.

[*Chapter 1:*] Epistle to the author's brother-in-law Juan, Archbishop of Toledo and Chancellor to the Crown, who is invited to consider, if he thinks it worthwhile, putting into Latin this plain work that consists (the author says) more of storytelling than fine reasoning (*más fabliella que muy buen seso*); he has previously (the author, i.e.) translated from Latin to Castilian a gloss or study of the Pater Noster by the Archbishop. Begun during sleepless nights in Sevilla, this work has grown out of his desire to turn his troubled mind from his cares, for God has not seen fit to let him satisfy his need to do Him some great service.

[*Chapter 2:*] Eulogy of knowledge, its acquisition and promotion through written works. Explanation that this book contains material adapted from other works (unnamed, but especially from one work in particular), as well as the author's original contributions. [The narrative begins:] "In the beginning of that other book there is mention of a wise and respected king . . ."

Chapter 3: [MS has only the title and two sentences.] An apprentice-knight seeking knighthood tires while journeying to a royal assembly convoked by the king and falls asleep astride his horse (which leads him to a retreat where an old knight lives a life of solitary meditation and penance).

Chapters 4–15: [Four missing folios delete these entirely.]

Chapter 16: [MS provides last eight sentences.] The old knight sketches for the boy the duties of kings as God's representatives.

Chapters 17–21: The aged knight discourses on society's basic division into the three strata of those who look after spiritual needs, those who maintain law and order, and those who produce and exchange material goods; the greatest single act a man can hope to perform occurs during the consecration of the mass; among the laity the highest level to be achieved is that of knighthood whose ritual is similar to that of the sacraments; the youth should consult Vegecio's complete treatise on chivalry; the major qualities a knight must achieve are those of being in the state of grace, using his reason (excursus: the four degrees of generosity and miserliness), and responding to his conscience; the greatest sorrow is to fail to be in a state of grace, while the greatest joy is to know that one is living in this state, since the specter of "Death walks with a man every step of every day."

Chapters 22–31: The discourse ceases and the frame takes over, as the youth is encouraged to seek knighthood; he is successful in this, after informing a pleased royal court of his encounter with the hermit-knigtht; after a visit to his homeland the just-dubbed *cavallero novel* again seeks the company and answers of the physically weak old man, whose discursive commentary will now run uninterrupted through eighteen chapters, while he protests constantly that he is without formal, classical training (*yo nunca leý nin aprendí ninguna sçiençia*) but has learned by associating with knowledgeable men (*para los legos non ha tan buena escuela en el mundo cuemo criarse omne et bevir en casa de los sennores*).

Chapters 32–39: The range of topics includes the nature of angels, heaven, hell, the eight revolving spheres of the universe, the four physical elements whose evolving masses will disintegrate at the time of the Parousia, the planets (astrology), and the concept of man as microcosm and as an inverted tree.

The digressions (which are digressions to us, not to Juan Manuel) are frequent and treat the inability of the human senses and brain to grasp supernatural concepts; the inadvisability of quick decisions and belated execution in crucial matters; the avoidance of doubt in matters of faith caused by not accepting on faith those doctrines beyond our comprehension; the four degrees on the psychological scale of bravery/fear; the human trait of making value judgments on the basis of second-hand information or according to the tenor of someone's remarks, rather than the cold facts themselves; the importance of carefully choosing the right teachers for one's children up to and after the age of fourteen; the uselessness of physically punishing children who have reached adolescence; the stupidity of believing that such qualities as bravery can be taught; the dependence of a smoothly functioning society on each person's awareness of and satisfaction with his way of life and its limitations; a catechism; etc.

At times the old man devotes only the last line or two of a set discourse to providing the definition called for; his protestations of ignorance in these matters are so repetitious they become unintentionally humorous, as in Chap. 37. Finally exasperated, he cautions the youth that he must scold him but will do so as father to son, for although "a father may punish his child with one hand, he feeds him with the other."

Chapters 40–48: This richly interesting section on natural history, the model for which could have come from several medieval and classical sources, treats in turn animals, reptiles, insects, etc., classified as killers or prey, etc.; birds, in a chapter marked with the author's personality, in which the old man (*vice* Juan

Manuel) is expert falconer and apologist for the sport, and in which the osprey has one webbed foot (*dizen que an un pie de águila et otro çerrado commo ánsar*) and migratory habits are carefully detailed; fish, with additional comment from an author acutely conscious of dietary questions (the most edible fish are small specimens with scales and much blood who live in unpolluted or nonmarshy sea water); wild grasses, which could be utilized more profitably, if only our scientific information on their properties were greater; trees, which are to be appreciated for aesthetic reasons as well as for their commercial value (the traveler who crosses the Tierra de Campos today, after noting the highland plain specimens in Juan Manuel's elaborate list of fifty trees and shrubs, may wonder what this region was like in the fourteenth century); stones, building and precious, even those found in roosters' gizzards and toads' skulls; minerals, perhaps engendered on earth by outer planetary forces; the ocean, with its salinity technically explained; the earth's crust, defined as support for all living things.

The pattern of at least one excursus per chapter is not often broken. The author's themes include the big talkers who do little (*muchos lo dizen de palabra, mas pocos lo fazen de fecho*); the four grades on the scale brilliant/stupid; an attack on the clients of sorcerers, alchemists, and counterfeiters (the latter an activity Juan Manuel will later take up himself in Villena and elsewhere in his financially desperate years in the late twenties and early thirties); the three reasons men live long lives and the three ways men die; the problems of why good men may die young and why guilty men may go unpunished; the disposition of legal matters by the proper authority and according to the proper code, an extremely sore point with the author (compare stanzas 142–47 of the *Book of Good Love* with Juan Manuel's similar insistence on the unrestricted judicial powers of the king, which here he extends to *grandes sennores*).

Chapters 49–51: The final question is directed to the youth, whose personality is momentarily usurped by the author to explain how in serious conflicts it is crucial to wait until one's opponent has clearly and publicly committed some wrong; and how the hours he devoted to study and reading had to be taken from those reserved for sleeping. Before returning home, the young knight agrees to remain with the old man in his final days and see to his burial.

One of the books evidently read by Don Juan on a sleepless night in Sevilla was Ramón Llull's *Llibre del orde de la cavaylería,* since from it he clearly borrowed (or surreptitiously stole, according to the chauvinist cries of some outraged protectors of Catalan integrity) the narrative frame of the hermit-knight and the youth. The considerable differences between the two books generally, however, have been sufficiently stressed in more objective analyses. This is not to deny the obvious influences of the Franciscan mystic on Don Juan Manuel, underscored by Lida de Malkiel,[1] but, as with the *Lucanor,* the broad path that seems to lead to his sources often begins felicitously (with St. Isidore, Alfonso X, etc.) but soon ends in a labyrinthine catalogue of guesswork possibilities, as Juan Manuel shapes characteristically in his own fashion the material that came his way. This work and the one next described (*Estados*) are Juan Manuel's primary contributions of an "encyclopedic" nature. In them he provides a world picture for his age that is unique in his century.

The sentiments of disdain for what he has written, expressed rhetorically in prefatory and other statements throughout his works (such as here in the preface to *Knight*), have been interpreted in various ways.[2] They provide one of those areas for conjecture that can be interesting in the case of a figure with Don Juan's personality. It is difficult to believe that he was ever seriously concerned for very long that his books would be harshly criticized, despite the internal evidence that could be amassed to support such an idea. Of course it occurred to him at some point that someone might ridicule his literary efforts; what really was on his mind, however, was not this but rather someone's not understanding what he was trying to do. He set for himself certain goals with what he thought were proper limitations, and he believed that he had achieved these goals. He was doubtless impressed with the learning he encountered among some prelates; this also must have been his reaction when around certain members of Jaime II's family. Such feelings, however, would not have invalidated his belief that he had accomplished something worthwhile. He certainly felt no sense of inferiority in the presence of the semiliterate and illiterate Castilian nobility of the fourteenth century. The Lara, Haro, los Cameros, and Castro males let their swords do their talking; and the Basque lines that would move upward in the next century (Guevara, Ayala, Mendoza, etc.) were at this point an impoverished, unschooled lot with greedy eyes on the south, awaiting the Trastámara upheaval.

II Libro de los estados (Book on the Plan of Society)

Considered his major contribution after the *Lucanor,* this long and strange work is not easily dealt with in its allotted space. One is tempted to attribute the paucity of critical attention paid it over the years to its availability in only the Gayangos and Benavides editions, yet this is scarcely sufficient in the face of its evaluation on two counts: It is said to provide the most thoroughly organized picture of social strata in the late Middle Ages, and it evolves its ideas through a curiously intertwined relationship (and even psychological give-and-take) between the characters and the author himself.[3] Don Juan Manuel is as concerned as ever with the artistic presentation and polishing of even the driest didactic text, and here the innovative techniques are striking: The creator of the text moves freely in and out of the train of thought and action; he converses with invented people; he accepts (!) their advice, becoming himself a fictional character manipulated in the third person by himself. What was least important to Juan Manuel in this work, i.e., the freely thrown-together fictional frame, has come to be what is most important to later scholars. Hence references to his use of the Barlaam and Josaphat story for his frame abound amid little concern for this extraordinary wealth of ideas and literary devices.

In the author's vision, and in that of most medieval men, society is ordered into *estados* or social groupings in each of which the individuals are characterized by distinctive social responsibilities, privileges, and legal status; this is the meaning of the word in the title. Although there are regular admonishments that the members of each *estado* must perform their functions dutifully and live out their lives happily in the *estado* to which they were born, it is decidedly overdramatic to see this work as a warning that wayward elements of society (usually with a religious background) are seeking to destroy the social order. This is not to say that Don Juan Manuel is not aware of the social impact of heretical ideas promoted in the low Middle Ages, but it is going too far, simply because he is orthodox even among the orthodox, to set him up as a target every time he puts pen to paper. Society has been permanently organized in a certain way for its own good, in the author's view, and this arrangement is not something that has come about fortuitously. The ideas he puts forth were prevalent long before his time and will persist long afterward; the student of this work would do well to begin with the *Siete Partidas,* the law compendium of the previous century. A summary of the contents of this rich and extraordinary work is obviously not possible here; indeed, such an undertaking would seem to have an air of inanity about it, and would be distasteful, were its result ever thought of as a substitute for reading the work itself. What follows is a mere enumeration and consideration of some of its features.

THE FIRST BOOK—Chapters 1–3: The Archbishop of Toledo is invited to read this work, on the organization of society and the religious creeds (*leyes*) men live by, for what it is worth and to correct its flaws. Its first book, written (the author says) during a time of great sorrow, treats laymen; its second, the clergy. Its schema is announced as one of questions and answers so as to make its presentation clear and understandable. The book proper begins (Chap. 3) by contrasting Mary's faith on Good Friday with the apostles' doubt. The Saturday Office of Our Lady sung most of the year commemorates (he believes) those moments before Sunday when mankind's faith lived in her alone, a faith which the miracle of the Pentecost would later cause to be preached to all peoples, even as it is still preached today.

The Barlaam Adaptation—Chapers 4–22: And so it was that an evangelist named Julio was preaching the good news in our times in a pagan land whose pagan king, Morabán, fearing that his son and heir Joas might be affected adversely by knowledge of death and the grief it brings, had instructed the boy's tutor, a knight named Turín, to keep such knowledge from the prince. Despite this Joas eventually sees a corpse and wailing funeral cortege and, shaken by the sight, demands and receives an explanation, which reveals the fact that humans have immortal souls as well as decaying bodies. Joas admits to earlier suspicions, having observed people's teeth fall out, their hair turn white, and children who seemed to appear out of nowhere; but now the young prince insists on knowing what manner of life on earth and what role in society will most effectively insure the salvation of his soul. [This question will constitute the central theme of the entire work, and the many expository digressions derive from or lead back to it.]

Joas' Religious Instruction—Chapters 23–40: Julio, learned and Christian, has become the lad's tutor; an earlier revelation of his (Chap. 20) has already caught the reader by surprise: He had been tutor to the son no less of the Infante Manuel and Beatriz of Savoy in the distant land of Castile (!), a lad who (he says) was later often embroiled in wars with the landed barons of Castile, as well as with the kings of Aragon and Granada. [With only occasional interruptions from the prince, and a rare word or two from Turín and Morabán, Julio's spoken instruction and advice on the makeup of society and the Christian solution to its problems will now take up the rest of the work, 126 chapters in all.] Julio believes that since mankind's needs are best served by acceptance of a set of religious beliefs, the problem is to determine the proper doctrine to accept. A discussion on the theological implications of natural law and revealed truth follows, and the Judeo-Christian tradition (*ley*), with references to the still viable Donation of Constantine and the rise of Islam, is sketched in a discourse by Julio that includes occasional commentary of a Thomistic bent on causality, the use of reason, the Almighty as Prime Mover, etc.

The Three Pagans Baptized—Chapters 41–46: Julio's counterbalancing Eve with Mary illustrates perfectly how the medieval church softened the terror of original sin with the gentle innocence of Mary, and the author has Joas select a day reserved in the Virgin's honor as the day of his conversion. The reader is now again startled (unless he knows from experience that this author has an irresistible urge to slip onto the page and join, or become, the people in the story) by the insertion of exact dates in October, 1328, for the christening of Joas as Juan and of Morabán as Manuel; the etyma and religious significance of these fine new names (Turín takes "Pedro") are elucidated. [In Chaps. 42 and 46, Don Juan Manuel interrupts the stream of dialogue that has run practically unbroken since Chap. 22, as the baptisms, etc., are narrated in the third person.] Julio's continuing instruction keys on the idea of renewal, or being born again, and touches on, among other things, the new (Christian) laws of fast and abstinence; penance; the taking of only one wife; and the substitution of the Consecration for blood sacrifice, and of baptism (a neater operation, he believes) for circumcision as the symbolic act of cleansing.

The Role of Emperor—Chapters 47–83: In this, the most interesting and richest section of the work by far in personal revelations and ideas, the main current running through Julio's instruction is that of assuaging the prince's doubts about an emperor's role in the secular world as it relates to his soul's salvation and to the conduct of his personal and public life while in office. It is pointed out that much of what is said may be applied also to those in the ranks of royalty and high nobility. There will be apologies from Julio later for relegating the clergy to the latter part of the work, the excuse being that this analysis of social roles is for the benefit of someone (Joas) who will serve his God and his society in a lay capacity. The baptisms concluded (the entire population is converted), the maintenence of some semblance of a developing fictional narrative no longer concerns the author. The figures and personalities of Julio and Joas are somewhat blurred and their commentary, though punctuated with requests and compliments from the prince, often flows as if from one mouth as Don Juan freely expounds on matters that interest him.

The abundance of concrete details on, and especially the concern for, the office of the papally-confirmed Roman Emperor, who is first "King of Germany" in Juan Manuel's words, may at first surprise the reader convinced of the political isolation of Castile: The seven Electors; the Emperor-elect's test in two actual sieges; the disastrous effects of a conflict between Pope and Emperor, who must harmonize like sun and moon and avoid ill-omened eclipses; the ideological confrontation symbolized in the Guelph-Ghibelline struggle; the promotion of an anti-Pope; the insistence that it is not the political system that fails but the misguided individual within it. [There is no mention of Alfonso X's imperial designs.] The Emperor is more important than most in the divine scheme of things, but not (as some would define the author's views) because as an individual his salvation is intrinsically more important, but because the role assigned to him is one from which may come great amounts of good or evil.

His eternal reward may be that much greater, or his damnation that much worse; all this, however, has nothing to do with his intrinsic merits, but rather derives from the fortuitous circumstance of his having to carry out a certain function in society. [This is a distinction that must be generally kept in mind, or the author's later statement, for example, that uneducated workers in town or field find themselves in extreme danger of losing their souls will be misread.] A clarification of the problems that accompany an Emperor's power and wealth is pursued in Chap. 55 with the explanation that the Gospel does not preach rewards for the man who is poor simply because he is not rich, but rather for that man who is poor by choice. Chap. 57 provides a sudden break in tempo, as the prince offers a fervent plea to mankind to recall what God-as-man was willing to suffer for its salvation. This is a remarkably passionate and incisively phrased sermon that one might imagine being intoned with subdued yet dramatic intensity by a master preacher from the house of San Pablo.

Personal reminiscences, often starkly realistic, are always present, since Juan Manuel was a man who forgot little: the not infrequent attempts on his life, especially after the deaths of the regents on the plain of Granada in 1319; the constant fear of being poisoned; the night in Villaóñez when he awoke to find the Infante Felipe and eight hundred armed horsemen there to kill him. Julio relates how "his good friend Don Johan" said that he reminded his brother-in-law Juan Núñez of the importance of utilizing a regular and productive schedule in one's daily activities; this remark follows a suggested dawn-to-dusk routine for the Emperor and dates this section after the 1329 marriage to Blanca Núñez. An idea of Juan Manuel's personality, as well as his personal habits, may be got from this constant flow of suggestions: An example at random counsels an Emperor who awakens at night to make plans for the future and to jot down the decisons reached so that no time is wasted the next day rethinking them. After a passage of detailed advice on the Emperor's household staff (the maids should not be too young or pretty, the wife must be given a decent budget, etc.) and the atmosphere to be maintained in the home (they must all love him, yet tremble before him), an extraordinary chapter (67) that may be the most quoted one in this work takes up his ideas on the education and upbringing of youth. In this chapter is also found the oft-quoted reference to the fact that his mother insisted on breast-feeding him (her only son) herself during his infant years and to his emotion at recalling her tell him this (she died before he was eight). The many vivid Spanish expressions with the word "milk" heard today sound a bit stronger after one has read this chapter.

Don Juan devotes ten chapters (70–79) to warfare. They constitute a substantial contribution that begins with a moving statement of his troubles with Alfonso XI and runs a rich gamut: extensive information on the use of walled positions, commando strikes, military intelligence, the notion of "cold war," the psychology of fear and noise-produced panic, spy systems, his delight with the use of a system of unextinguishable lamps for night treks, etc. These chapters are sometimes referred to with a statement of Don Juan's respect and high praise for the Moslem warrior, but, while there is no denying this, what may be said first is that his comments are also simply the objective reporting of things he has seen himself. And the Moslem is not without his problems in the field: He already has a special dread for the Castilian crossbowman, as well as the foot soldier—the same Spanish infantryman who will be the scourge of Europe two centuries later. Curiously, yet quite characteristically, the author allows *himself* to be quoted directly (Chap. 70) with a reference, accompanied by a chuckle, to his successes in secret diplomacy. He hammers at the fact that there is no hope for a Christian cavalry troop that breaks ranks; the Moslem "game" of *torna-fuy* (mock flight) is played with perfection to draw out and scatter the Christian forces, and in any running battle on horseback the Moslem is deadly. Some of the author's sentiments have a familiar ring: What is to be feared most is fear itself; no one really wins at war; among a war's "heroes" thought to have enjoyed martyrdom's reward are pillagers and rapists; the fact that postwar excesses are as criminal and brutal a problem as those during the conflict itself, etc.

The Roles of Titled-Class Protectors—Chapters 84–91: The thirteen ranks here classified range through Kings, Crown Princes, noninheritable Infantes, sons of Infantes (like Don Juan Manuel), Dukes, Marquises, *Príncipes,* Counts, Viscounts, *Ricosomnes, Infanzones,* Knights, and Apprentice-Knights; all are *fijosdalgo.* This concludes the major portion of the work devoted to the keepers of the peace or *defensores,* in this typically trilevel stratification. The status in which one faces the greatest danger of failing to meet his earthly obligations and thereby losing his soul is that held by Don Juan Manuel himself, a reasonable assumption expected in this book if one has taken the time to review everything this author has written about himself and his salvation. This rank of *fijo de infante* is the subject of a remarkable interlude in Chap. 85: The author here recalls an intimate meal and conversation with the Archbishop of Santiago, Rodrigo del Padrón, who, "in his Galician language," warned him of the corrupt pattern of existence into which Infantes' sons seemed generally doomed to fall. Chap. 87 strikes to the heart of circumstances that bitterly involved Don Juan on more than one occasion: it establishes those cases in which a fief-holder (*vassallo*) or native citizen (*natural*) has the right to deny his feudal obligation to his baron. Don Juan Manuel the linguist is as fond as ever of providing his public with a gratuitous lesson or two and does so especially in Chap. 89, which is replete with etymologies (of which the most mind-boggling is that of "infante") and a semantico-structural analysis of adjective distribution in *ricoomne* and *omne rico.*

The Roles of Non-Titled Protectors and Those of the Land-Working/Mercantile/Artisan Class—Chapters 92–98: A sharply detailed panorama of fourteenth-century society is presented with an array of civil servants, professional soldiers, and public officials, followed by a five-chapter (94–98) disquisition on the duties of the professional servants and officials who function in the houses of their overlords: The accountant or *mayordomo,* the tutor, the first secretary and intimate counsellor (*chanceller*), the physician, the personal or body servant (*camarero*), the *despensero* who oversees the day-to-day purchases, etc. These are all generally grouped with the *defensores,* leaving little to be said of the food-producing and goods-producing and exchanging level of society, all classed as *labradores.* Curiously, in view of his continuing difficulties as Adelantado in Murcia, Don Juan sees fit to lament at some length the perversion of justice that may occur in this office (*merinos* and *adelantados* dispense justice by royal appointment over large stretches of territory, within which the local power to detain people and enforce local ordinances in towns, villages, castles, etc., rests with an *alcalde* or *alguacil*). The modern reader of these chapters, even though familiar with the horrors of the twentieth century, is unfailingly shaken by the stress here on the quick application of laws that often involve some form of mutilation or slow starvation. The plea in Chap. 93 that justice must do more than punish the guilty (it should, he believes, find ways of rewarding a citizen's outstanding service) is sincere, but swift and, more importantly, *visible* reprisal is always the fourteenth-century solution to the disturbance at hand, as when Bartolomé Zanón was accused of speaking impudently before Don Juan in Murcia in 1329 and had his tongue cut out. The medicine for social ills receives no clearer expression than that given earlier by Don Juan: When one is called to a disturbance and finds that the instigator has killed someone, he should arrange for the burial of the live man in a coffin beneath that of the dead man. This will get the message across.

All Secular Roles as a Unit Concluded—Chapters 99–100: The midpoint colophon announces the place (Pozancos, just north of Sigüenza) and date (May 22, 1330) of completion, just seventeen days (he says) after his forty-eighth birthday.

THE SECOND BOOK—Chapter 1: Expressing concern over the increased difficulty in taking up the ecclesiastical sphere, the author finds inspiration in the fact that the liturgical season is presently that of Pentecost. This second book is provided with a customary presentation, invocation, lamentation over its flaws, etc.; hence the author addresses it again (he has no choice) to the Infante, who is called Patriarch of Alexandria. This title, prestigious though largely honorary (nonelective, unlike other Patriarchates), does not indicate a time lapse after the completion of the first book since it had been conferred in 1328.[4]

The Role of the Clergy as a Group—Chapters 2–8: [The prince will interrupt his tutor on only a few brief occasions in the last forty-eight chapters, and only a bare phrase or two now and then indicates that a dialogue is taking place.] Carrying out the highest role man can fulfill on earth, the clergy is the foundation on which rests the creed, and they must defend it against fellow Christian, Jew, Moslem, and pagan. The mysteries in the Christian interpretation must be approached (he says) the way a man warms himself by the fire: If he insists on getting at the source, he will be burned; if he strays too far away, he perishes in the cold. The author is quick to admit that the Bible appears to contradict itself, and that the intellectual who struggles to grasp the mystery will lose his soul with much more facility than the uneducated. Despite all this, Juan Manuel is concerned above all with urging a clear, convincing presentation of the Christian solution to the nonbeliever. That anyone would reject it, after being made aware of the symmetry of its doctrine, is something he always ultimately finds hard to believe. By his admonition to avoid formal arguments on matters of faith with learned nonbelievers, he gives evidence of having debated religious questions himself, or of having heard such debates possibly from Dominicans, who must have come out none too well. These discussions may have taken place with disputatious Christians and Jews, and even with Moslems knowledgeable in both faiths (*algunos moros muy sabidores*) who are mentioned in Chap. 3.

In a strange paragraph (Chap. 4) he warns that cryptic lettering (or shorthand?) will be used when necessary to prevent the untrained from misinterpreting his remarks; blank lines, such as those in Chap. 7, indicate that these passages were not copied, at least not in the only surviving manuscript. An abrupt invitation is extended to see the author personally (!) in cases of doubt.

Apologetics (continued) and Christian Symbolism—Chapters 9–32: Chap. 8 lists the topics for the next twenty-three chapters, and, beginning with the sixth age of mankind, in which Christ appeared on earth, they present a symbolistic interpretation of events relating to his birth (9–17), life (18–21), and Passion-Resurrection (22–30). Chap. 31 describes the Christian Passover and its complementary feast, the descent of the Holy Ghost, as the fulfillment of events prefigured in the Jewish tradition: the sacrifice of the paschal lamb, the giving of the law on Sinai, etc.

The Role of the Pope—Chapters 33–42: The author's characteristic concern over organizing his materials is apparent in his prelisting of the hierarchy, from Pope down through the mendicant orders, the Augustinians, the *monges blancos et prietos,* who are Cistercians (not Cistercians and Benedictines), and the military orders: Castilian (Santiago, Calatrava, Alcántara, and the Hospitallers of St. John); Aragonese (that of Montesa, endowed by the author's father-in-law with Templar holdings); and Portuguese (the recently founded Order of Christ with its

Templar properties, and that of Aviz, or the Portuguese Cala-trava). The status of the Papacy and especially the problems inherent in such great temporal and spiritual powers are taken up at length.

The Church Hierarchy—Chapters 43–47: The description pro-ceeds through the ranks of Cardinal, Patriarch, Archbishop, Bishop, Abbot, Dean (of cathedral canons), through the posts attached to cathedral and collegiate chapters, down to village priests (*capellanes*). Don Juan is curiously concerned with recon-ciling the contemplative and active forms of devotion, and, as is to be expected, with restoring the peninsular primacy of the Archbishopric of Toledo. He reserves a bitter condemnation for any ordained cleric, from Pope to country priest, who conse-crates the host when not in the state of grace: "When I see that he has the servant woman with him at night, and fouls his hands and his mouth, and his very person that is to offer up the sacri-fice of the mass [. . .]"

Eulogy of the Order of Preachers—Chapter 48: The reasons for the author's attachment to the Dominicans have been made clear all along: They do what he thinks must be done. Preaching, teaching, confessing, they take the Word to the people. Although he has kind words for the Franciscans, his greatest praise is for the friars of the strict rule founded by the Spaniard from Cale-ruega, "whence came the flower of the line of Guzmán." His Ca-stilian nationalism runs strong in this long final chapter on the life of Dominic (whose mother's tomb is at San Pablo in Peña-fiel) and the practices of his foundation.

III   Libro infinido (The Unfinished Book)

Written, according to its prologue, for his two-year-old son Fernando (by Blanca Núñez, b. 1332?) who "requested" of him a book, this personalized compendium of nobleman's advice has as its stated purpose the relation of things the author has lived through and seen for himself (*cosas que yo prové et bi*). Don Juan plans the addition of guidelines that his future experiences will reveal to him: hence the title, meaning "open-end." The twenty-six chapters, drawing heavily on *Estados*, especially after Chap. 8, and with many explicit references to this work, have the appearance of a series of formal, paternal epistles: *Fijo don Ferrando[. . .]* Compared often to Sancho IV's *Castigos (Counsel) y documentos,* a work similarly addressed to a son, the *Unfinished Book* reveals a Juan Manuel for once (biblical mentions aside) exact in one of his rare references to classical and medieval authors: "Fray Gil" = Egidio Colonna, Chap. 4. As Lida de Malkiel has shown, such indications from him are usually vague and lead nowhere.[5]

After an initial chapter, the longest of the first twenty-five, on the care of his son's soul (go to confession frequently even before you are old enough to sin, ask the Prior Provincial for a suitable confessor, etc.), and two chapters of counsel on his physical well-being and the upbringing of noble youth, the following eleven chapters (4–14) deal with personal relationships. They set forth a code of conduct for his son that is geared to an awareness of his high station, a station the father does not wish undermined in either the near or distant future. The range covered is broad, from the king and other nobles to his immediate family and personal servants. The message in a given chapter can be dispensed in short order, such as Chap. 5's declaration on noblemen in Spain of greater status than his son: There are none. He openly threatens to reject his son (Chap. 9), with a curse (*so pena de la mi bendición*) the full weight of which might be underestimated today, should the boy discharge or mistreat the family's present loyal retainers.

His son's public stance and his comportment in public and personal matters are the topics for Chaps. 15–25: the judicious handling of confidential information, the need for maintaining fortified strongholds, etc., all topics discussed earlier in *Estados* and given summary treatment here. Chap. 26 breaks somewhat with the tenor of the book up to that point. The Dominican Prior at Calatayud has asked him to write on the kinds of *amor* that are possible between people. After a much quoted defense of his propensity for literature ("I believe my time better spent writing books than rolling dice and in other idle games"), he defines fifteen types of *amor* that run a broad gamut of relations between men (not men and women) from one that is absolutely unselfish and never observed by him (*este amor yo nunca lo vi fasta oy*) to a pretended "love" that is a cover-up for deception.[6]

The personal note that one comes to expect is here abundantly present in the first seven chapters: the insomnia he believes an inherited family affliction; his insistence that his son give preference, as he always did, to the Zag family over other Jewish families with a tradition in medicine; his obsession with diet: the rigid dicta on wine (when and how diluted it should be drunk, but no indication, unfortunately, of his preferred grape or where it matured). A thousand horses take the field at his command, and every night on a journey from Navarra to Granada may be spent in a castle or walled town that is Manueline property. There are even instructions on the seating of specific house guests: The Haro and Lara barons go well above the salt, more so than the clans of Los Cameros and Castro.

CHAPTER 6

The Virgin in Heaven and Falcons over the Júcar

MASS at daybreak and a clear cold sky over the Segura or Duero basin for an early morning ride to the hawks; a day spent in counsel and meetings, carefully organized toward maximum decision-making with the use of notes jotted down in a sleepless hour the night before; a day divided by brief moments of meditation, perhaps on Mary's bodily presence in heaven, during the singing of Terce and None, the latter preceded by the obligatory nap to counteract those foods that go to one's head; the beneficial evening exercise, to "change the air," that precedes Vespers and a meal enlivened with the conversation of the two Calatayud friars and the baron from Aragon; the minstrel, his vielle, and his tale of Fernán González at Hacinas, are followed by more stimulating conversation; and late into the night the sleepless hours are turned to the outlining, composition, and correction of works, pleasurable tasks interrupted only by nagging thoughts on the severity of his insomnia this night. If the reader becomes too immersed in the individual periods of conflict in the life of Don Juan Manuel that absorb practically the totality of his typical biography, and then fits that into the black aura of despair with which the historian coats Spain's fourteenth century, he might come to believe that a day like the one described could only have been a rarity in the life of Don Juan Manuel. And this would not be the case, since the greater part of his life was doubtless spent in just such fashion.

I Libro de la caza (Book on Hunting)

The following passages, from Chapters 8 and 12 of Juan Manuel's *Libro de la caza*, provide a brief sample of the author's richly personal and anecdotal manner in this work.

But Don Johan tells a story he thinks most unusual of a saker he once saw, called "Prelado" and owned by the Infante Johan. On a chase one day up toward León on the Bernesga river, with the saker on the arm of a falconer named Pero Nuñes, he and the Infante sighted a pair of heron and first released another sorry saker held by the falconer Garcya Ferrandiz; after they were well up and climbing, the falconer Ferrant Gomes set off a peregrine belonging to Don Johan that could hardly be seen by the time he overtook and crippled one of the prey; after both peregrine and victim were on the ground, the remaining heron was so high it looked scarcely larger than a dove. They then let fly that saker of the Infante Johan, and it reached the prey so quickly the strike could be seen. Now Don Johan's best estimate would be to guess that if the heron was at, say, a height of 15,000 measures and climbing, the saker hit it before it went another thousand. But the incredible fact is not that the kill was achieved at such a height, for Don Johan has released many a falcon that took its prey so high they could not be seen, but that the saker mounted this long climb at such an unbelievable rate of speed, a feat he had never witnessed before by either gyrfalcon or peregrine or saker. (Chap. 8)

And the story has been told of a count in Portugal named Gonçalo Garcia, who would clip the wing and tail feathers of young peregrines before their first molting, and fit them out with leg bands and tinkling bells. Thus decorated they had the run of the house their first year, mingling with man, dog, and chicken. Then when they began to molt, he set up a cage for them in the yard for that purpose; and after they had molted, he trained them to take heron and never any other game. (Chap. 8)

And Villena is splendid for taking every kind of game, the best there is in all of Murcia. And Don Johan goes so far as to say that he has seen few places its equal for sheer variety, for even from the top of its castle one can see heron, mallard, and crane taken with falcon or goshawk; as well as partridge and quail, hare and rabbit, and even those birds called flamingos, beautiful birds, easy to hunt but difficult to retrieve since they prefer large saltwater lagoons. Likewise from the castle itself the hunting of boar, deer, and wild goat can be observed; Don Johan has participated in such hunts himself within eyesight of the castle. He claims killing boar so close that he could be recognized from the castle. And except for the great quantities of eagles in the area and an occasional severe gorge nearby he would say that this was the best hunting terrain he had ever seen. (Chap. 12)

The stream running through the vicinity of Santa María del Campo has its source above the village and empties into the Cañabate [Rus] right by Villar de Cantos [. . .] and between the [Garcimuñoz] castle and El Cañabate near Montiella there are two lagoons excellent for taking wild duck with falcons, but if one hunts bustards there he is in for a handsome treat: Don Johan with his hawks and his men took over four hundred there in one day. (Chap. 12)

Between the Záncara river and Villar de la Encina there is a great lagoon [. . .] and with him there one day in the spring were Johan, son of Don Alfonso [X], Johan Rodrigues de Villalovos, Johan Velez de Vegara, and many other men and youth. And while they were crossing the lagoon in skiffs that day, in order to hunt bustards, a young peregrine attacked a prey in the latter's nest, and was carried away as the seized bird took flight with the other's talons still in it. Both were caught, still locked together, and brought to Don Johan, who after they reached camp picked up the young hawk in his hand. And whenever it saw the other bird, it seized it, gripping it by the leg so that it could not fly away. And Don Johan knows that if he were to give every detail of this exactly as it happened, it would scarcely be believable, but he knows what happened and it is the truth. Astonishing things occur when men hunt, and when they relate them, those not taken with the sport say that they are telling tall tales and are lying in their teeth. (Chap. 12)

But those streams that feed a mud flat or soft marshland, or that have steep banks even though they are not wide, these are places where sometimes you might make it through and sometimes you have a spill [. . .] and Don Johan even admits that he often thought it great sport to surprise his hunting companions by having them stumble or wander into such a place as a practical joke. And when nothing else worked, he would rush on ahead to the spot where he said they usually made the crossing; and after he had made them think that he was ready to go on through himself, and that he wanted them to get on ahead of him, in would they charge only to have their horses tumble or stagger around a bit as they sank in, and everyone would have a hearty laugh. And this he thinks is part of the fun of the hunt. But the joke should never be played where there is possible danger to man or beast. And he admits he is disappointed when they are on to his plan, those who know him for his pranks. (Chap. 12)

The reader may not be prepared at this point to think of Don Juan Manuel as the jolly practical joker; Don Juan has seldom been portrayed as the life of the party. The inclusion of the last paragraph above in his book on hunting is an indication itself of his enjoyment of these episodes. And the third item makes interesting reading after one has reached the ruins astride the hill of San Cristóbal.

The selections above give only an unsatisfactory, yet typical, glimpse of this technical, yet richly subjective work on the art and sport of taking game with birds of prey. The author's fascination with it may be gauged by the references to it in other works (tale 33 in *Count Lucanor*, e.g.), by his desire to extol its educational and utilitarian benefits, and by his eagerness to defend himself against criticism of the amount of time he devoted to it. If read after his other works have been considered, this book's style and the presentation of its data may appear awkward at times; overall there is the impression of a vigorous prose that rolls along in spontaneous and unpolished fashion. It would seem clearly one of his first works (early or mid-1320's), although Giménez Soler places it in the late 1330's. The literature on this most classical of the medieval nobleman's diversions is extensive; few such treatises have apparently been executed with a touch so personal as that of Juan Manuel. Other late medieval works on hunting produced in the peninsula, and generally brought up with the mention of this one, are those of Alfonso XI, Pero López de Ayala (who recalls Don Juan Manuel's prowess in this field), and Juan de Sahagún. "Hunting" (*caza*), more often than not, means simply falconry (*caza de aves*) in such works.

Beginning with a strong eulogy of Alfonso X, Juan Manuel's *Book on Hunting* generally splits its twelve chapters into three of classification and description; five on care, training, and current practices; three on problems related to molting, feeding, and diseases; and a long final chapter that is a remarkable falconer's guidebook to the bishoprics of Cartagena, Cuenca, and Sigüenza. A geographer's delight, it charts the terrain by stream and by shoreline, taking up the various game to be found, their feeding habits, the seasonal and migratory patterns, and providing such culinary tips as the fact that Cuenca partridges are much tastier than the Cartagena variety. For the province of Cuenca, at least, Don Juan furnishes in the course of his commentary what amounts to a veritable hydrologic survey of the region.[1]

The aesthetic quality of a falcon's performance is what counts: the drawn out series of soaring strikes by which certain species gradually bring down their prey results in a dramatic ritual that is more spectacular than that provided by others who quickly maim with constant claw pressure. Many birds were imported, often by sea, we are told, and Sardinia is indicated as one source.

The Virgin in Heaven and Falcons over the Júcar

The saker, however, could be taken wild or retrieved from its nests near Toledo and Salamanca, and as far north as Mayorga. The acquisition of a pure white gyrfalcon from Scandinavia must have been a moment of high excitement. The best hunter Juan Manuel believes he ever knew was the Infante Juan, who, in their long, agreeable conversations on the subject, often talked of the love of Juan Manuel's father for the sport and his fine stable of birds. For one excursion in Medellín the Infante Manuel supplied one hundred sixty hawks. The fascinating dissertation on diseases and medical care (*de las purgas e de las melezinas*) mentions the author's success at cauterizing wounds and a "white salve" of his own invention. He makes no absolute guarantees and even suggests that medicines be avoided if at all possible, but he has cured worms by forcing a lump of crystallized sugar (*açucar candio*) down the throat of the falcon, and he has closed wounds with dried human excrement (*estiercol del moço chico que mama*).

A medieval didactic treatise as lively as this one in its vivid relation of personal experiences would be difficult to find. It is valued as a rich source for lexical studies. Its author is concerned with the overall plan and the development of his subject, and more than one critic has called attention to his desire to elaborate technical information in a manner that he considers artistically pleasing.

II Tractado de la Asunçión (Essay on the Assumption)

In the presence of Don Juan some learned people commented on the fact that not everyone professing Catholicism believed in the bodily presence of Mary in heaven; these remarks, he tells us, took place at her mid-August feast called "en Castiella Sancta Maria de agosto mediado." The Assumption, not defined as dogma until 1950, was a debatable doctrine, especially in the early Middle Ages, as the mere fact of Juan Manuel's having written this treatise makes clear. He addresses it to his trusted confidant, Remón Masquefa, Prior of the Peñafiel Preachers, and seeks to show in a series of brief arguments that are largely rhetorical questions why the corporeal ascent must be logically believed in: Not to do so would be illogical. This short piece was evidently one of the last things he wrote.[2]

[127]

III Libro de las armas (Book on the Coat of Arms)

This brief treatise on Don Juan's and his family's history is at times given the more appropriate and convenient title *Libro de las tres razones (The Three Topics)*. The three items, the historical circumstances and meaning of which are the meat of this triad of essays, are (1) the origin and symbolic interpretation of the Manueline blazon; (2) the historical antecedents that permit him and his legitimate firstborn son to confer knighthood despite never having been knighted themselves; and (3) an account of the last words a twelve-year-old Juan Manuel heard from Sancho IV not long before the latter's death. A unifying thread of purpose throughout is one that casts in a favorable light his own heritage and family background while underscoring the desperate character of the blood line on the Castilian throne. Don Juan will claim vigorously, nevertheless, that he has served the son and grandson of Alfonso X as loyally as he could, but the bitterness wells up strongly with the mention of the current monarch.

A brief but rich panorama of late thirteenth-century Castilian and Aragonese history is presented here, at times gaudy and intimate in its detail. The first, and least interesting, of the three sections begins with a discussion of his father's birth and baptism in Carrión, both auspicious events presaging the grandeur of the name Manuel, after which the details of his upbringing are contrasted with "the senseless luxury wasted on royal children today." Then the family emblem, an example of which may be seen in San Pablo (maintained by Passionists) in Peñafiel today, is interpreted. The shield's red and white fields display golden wings with fist-held swords, and the clawing lions of León, respectively.

The author's point in his second essay is to illustrate how the primogeniture rights to Murcian territory endow each firstborn son of the line of Manuel with the right to bestow knighthood, a right, he pompously observes, not possessed by other descendants of infantes. The embroiled story of the Murcia-Alicante region is told with an array of specific and often intriguing detail for the political historian to ponder. The hatred of one of Jaime the Conqueror's daughters for her younger, prettier sister has its consequences: The older child, Violante, Queen of Castile as Alfonso X's wife, persuades her father to go against his word to marry the younger girl to Alfonso's brother Enrique, who is the classic reprobate of the period; Violante pleads, after a dramatic, incognito journey to see her father in Calatayud, that her kingdom will be lost if her sister comes to Castile as the wife of the heir next in line; she suggests that her sister might marry another brother, Manuel, to whom Murcia, about to be reconquered, may be given, and that there in faraway Murcia she and Manuel might well live happily ever after. The nuptial mass of Juan Manuel's father and his first wife, Constanza, is then celebrated in a church in Calatayud guarded by a hundred armed men poised against any intrusion from Enrique, and Manuel is granted permanent rights to territories around Elche. They decide to make their home in Castile, however, and when Constanza dies unexpectedly, the rumor spreads that she was poisoned by cherries received as a gift from her sister. The historian's first concern, after an initial exuberance over this unusual and intimate memoir, is to separate fiction, if such is present, from fact, a task made exceedingly difficult by the scarcity of corroborative documentation from the period.[3]

The impressionable meeting with the tubercular Sancho IV took place in the convent of Dominican nuns in Madrid, Santo Domingo el Real, in the late winter or early spring of 1295. Sancho "the Fierce" would cough for the last time in Toledo on April 25, 1295, and ten days later Juan Manuel would be thirteen years old. The ominous rumble of Basque insurrection at Sancho's impending death, the dreadful seizure suffered by the dying man at Quintanadueñas early in 1294, the contrasting vigorous youth of the author himself at that time, fresh from a victorious encounter of his men in Almería—all serve as prelude pieces carefully fitted together by Don Juan in the preparation of a suitable stage on which the once bold monarch might bare his remorseful soul. The scene is gradually permitted to narrow to the room in the Madrid convent, with the smell of death all about. And in the presence of only such intimate associates as his physician Abrahán, and Alfonso García, the boy's inseparable mentor, and Master Gonzalo, the Abbot of Arbás, the broken man on the bed finally turns to the boy and begins to talk. His father's dying curse against his son, repeating San Fernando's wrath a generation earlier, his plea that María de Molina not be left unaided after his death, his memory of the last days of San Fernando and the latter's gift of sword and blazon to his youngest son Manuel, his abject despair—all these things and others, broken only by agonized attempts to clear his diseased lungs for once and breathe, are uttered by the wracked figure frightened at the eternity before him. Sancho calls the young Juan to him for what will be a last farewell to the lad, wondering if a man so cursed as he can give a final blessing.[4]

This scene is a literary achievement the equal of which will not be observed in Spanish prose for another century and a half. And after all the personal and political judgments have been made, and he has been damned to everyone's content, let Don Juan Manuel here be given his due: No writer in medieval Spain knows so well as he knows here that the cold fact, in this case a dying man and his tortured soul, is not enough, and indeed will not stand by itself, and that if it is to have any meaning at all, the words must somehow be made to convey the dramatic essence of its inner truth.

To make much over the legendary and hearsay nature (always reported by the author as such) of some of the incidents brought up by Don Juan (his paternal grandmother's dreams when pregnant with his father and with his uncle, Alfonso el Sabio; the miracles attendant on the death of the sister of his father's first wife, an Aragonese Infanta who died unknown toiling in a pilgrims' hostel), and to allow Don Juan's fascination with such detail to color substantially one's view of the entire document, may serve to place it out of focus. The author begins this work by confessing to the Dominican Prior who, he says (again utilizing the ready motif of the "requested work"), has asked him to put in writing some things that came up in a conversation, that chatting about these matters in a free and friendly fashion is one thing, but that choosing the right words to put them in writing is a much more serious task. Juan Manuel's misgivings are made clear, not only repeatedly as he begins this piece, but throughout, and then again at the end. And while he states that this is the truth as nearly as he can determine, he is telling the reader in so many words that he *knows* that this or that detail will be questioned. He carefully stresses the secondhand nature of many of his remarks, and it is hardly proper to accuse him of deliberate falsification. Even on the *cause célèbre* of the suspected poisoning of his father's first wife, Don Juan does not state as fact that Alfonso X's wife murdered her younger sister. His point is that this is what people believed, this is what they said happened.

CHAPTER 7

Conclusion

D ON Juan Manuel will always be read not only for the delight in relishing his creative contribution to fiction, but with an interest that is multiple: discovering the man himself, his personality and his psyche, constructing the fourteenth-century world alive in his works, determining concretely his place in the development and perfection of peninsular and European prose. Despite his already substantial position in literary manuals, students of this writer are beginning to examine his art from different and more universal perspectives, and they are determining that his contribution is even greater than thought previously, in the establishment of a new awareness of artistic prose and the narrative art. And one of the crucial considerations in any estimate of Don Juan and his place in medieval Castilian prose is, apart from his ability to write so well, the fact that this man, in these extraordinary circumstances, felt so strongly moved to express himself, moved to innovative literary creation, and that he was able to accomplish this in a manner so markedly personal. This surely underscores decisively this moment in the history of peninsular prose and portends the rich tradition to follow.

As with some other medieval works, most notably the *Book of Good Love,* the work of Don Juan Manuel has occasionally been examined by students and scholars with preconceived, ready-made opinions on the nature and bias of its contents. This appears, however, to be a situation that has begun to change substantially. In the work of a number of interested scholars, among them British, Italian, and Latin-American specialists particularly, new approaches to the study of Don Juan Manuel are being marked out and clarified. The pairing and contrast with Juan Ruiz are almost inevitable, both for chronological as well as for other reasons. Both are felt to play highly visible roles in their works, and, despite the interminable conjecturing about the

Archpriest, they are both among those writers the reader, perhaps too easily, imagines he knows well. It may be even more important in the case of Juan Manuel that one not overreact to initial impressions when he comes face to face with the author on the written page. (It is not difficult to imagine these two crossing paths in Alcalá or Toledo, and Juan Manuel also knew the Alcarria well; surely some fine morning in Cifuentes or Hita or Brihuega he attended a mass, with no homily, celebrated by Juan Ruiz.)

As interest in Juan Manuel increases, perhaps it will at least approach the enthusiasm accorded the Archpriest in the last three decades. Although serious lacunae exist—a complete critical edition of the *Lucanor,* a definitive biography, a major thematic analysis of his use of folk, legendary, and historical materials, etc.—it will eventually become clear that Don Juan has much more to tell us, and tell us honestly, than any other peninsular writer in the low Middle Ages. Future studies of Don Juan Manuel may well address themselves not only to measuring his art as a composite of Greco-Roman, Semitic, and other medieval strains, but also toward what this man, at this time and in this place, individually accomplished.

Notes and References

Chapter One

1. Don Juan Manuel is often incorrectly titled Infante. His father was an Infante; Infantes and Infantas are the legitimate sons and daughters of kings. These terms serve as integral parts of the medieval name and will be so used in this study. Juan Manuel is also designated *príncipe* in some Spanish studies; *príncipe* is a term with broad semantic coverage in the fourteenth century as Don Juan himself explains in *Estados* (*Plan of Society*) I, 88. Juan Manuel's full name in fourteenth-century Spanish is usually written *Don Johan fijo del Infante Don Manuel*; *fijo* means "son." The name Manuel is here in the low Middle Ages in the process of becoming stabilized as a patronymic; Don Juan Manuel may be found catalogued under "Juan" or "Manuel," although the former is usually preferred.

The debt of these initial chapters to Andrés Giménez Soler, *Don Juan Manuel* (Zaragoza, 1932) cannot be adequately expressed. Where I have added to his remarks or corrected a minor point I have generally done so utilizing the documents in his work. A few details in Chapters 1 and 2 are further substantiated by documents in Vol. II of Antonio Benavides, *Memorias de D. Fernando IV de Castilla* (Madrid, 1860). All historians of early fourteenth-century Castile, however, including Giménez Soler, rely heavily at times on the *Chronicle of Alfonso XI*, of which several versions exist and whose veracity may be questioned when the details are not substantiated elsewhere. I have indicated in certain instances such unconfirmed parts of the narration.

2. A recent assessment is that of John E. Keller, *Alfonso X el Sabio* (New York: Twayne Publishers, Inc., 1967).

3. The Infante is the brother of King Dinis of Portugal. Juan Manuel mentions his half-sister's death in a letter to Jaime II (Giménez Soler, p. 341); he does not refer to it in any of his works. It is likely that after the deaths of both parents, Don Juan and Yolante, as her name usually appears in correspondence, were raised together as wards of Sancho IV. The Portuguese king explained his sister-in-law's

death in a letter to Jaime II (Giménez Soler, p. 342) saying that she was sickly and had confessed and composed her will, but even in this letter Dinis indicates that everyone believes his brother murdered her.

4. The reference is to Don Juan Manuel's *Libro de las armas;* see the list of his works on p. 59. In similar fashion, throughout this book, a title in parentheses indicates a work by Don Juan, unless otherwise specified. As stated earlier, the edition utilized in each case is the first one of that work listed in the Bibliography. Page references are provided to *Armas;* chapters are indicated in other works. The *Libro de los estados* is divided into first (I) and second (II) books.

5. The details may be consulted in any standard Spanish history: García de Valdeavellano, Suárez Fernández, Valdeón Baruque, Soldevila, Ballesteros, Vicens Vives, Altamira, Aguado Bleye, etc. Authors of recent histories in English are W. C. Atkinson, L. Bertrand-C. Petrie, and H. Livermore.

6. The Infante Enrique, Alfonso el Sabio's brother, plays a continually meddlesome role in politics until his death in Roa in 1303. The Infante Juan, Alfonso's son, is also vigorously active politically. Enrique is Juan Manuel's uncle; Juan is his first cousin. The former sided with the Cerda faction against Fernando IV; the latter favored Fernando and María de Molina and was the person most responsible for bringing the parties together at Agreda, Campillo, etc., in 1304 to agree on the Murcia question. Both will be mentioned in Don Juan Manuel's works: Enrique in the *Lucanor* (tale 9), Juan as the best falconer he ever knew in the *Book on Hunting*, etc., etc. The Infante Juan is the same Juan who, with Moslem troops at Tarifa's walls in 1294, killed Guzmán el Bueno's son; Juan Manuel will have him delightfully described by Sancho IV in *Armas* as that wretch hell-bent in the south: *aquel pecador del infante don Johan que anda perdido en tierra de moros.* Readers of Tirso de Molina's *Prudencia en la mujer* are already familiar with these figures.

7. The Sancho Manuel mentioned is Don Juan Manuel's illegitimate half-brother.

8. The chronicles or royally mandated histories of the reigns of Alfonso X, Fernando IV, and Alfonso XI are mentioned at times in this study. They are edited in the *Biblioteca de Autores Españoles:* see note 1 in Chapter 2 below.

Chapter Two

1. This particular period has long had a special reputation as one of the most disastrous intervals of political history in Castile. It has often been characterized by a remarkable passage in the *Chronicle of Alfonso XI* that describes the beginnings of social revolt, uprisings of farm workers, a countryside glutted with bands of roving thieves and

cutthroats. Towns not walled are empty of people, and it is not thought strange to see corpses along the roads. *Crónicas de los Reyes de Castilla*, I, in *BAE* (*Biblioteca de Autores Españoles*), Madrid, 1953, Vol. 66, 197.

2. H. T. Sturcken, "The Assassination of Diego García by Don Juan Manuel," to appear in *Kentucky Romance Quarterly* (1973–1974).

3. This situation may seem peculiar: Don Juan is now joining forces with the Portuguese king who earlier had deceived him and whose daughter Alfonso XI chose to marry while rejecting Constanza; also Don Juan is complaining to the King of Castile that he is not honoring his legitimate spouse, whom Don Juan did not want him to marry in the first place. Don Juan's rejections of Alfonso XI as his sovereign are not procedures devised out of thin air; they are recognized legal steps, and Don Juan discusses them in *Estados* I, 86.

4. Constanza bore Pedro three children before he became infatuated with Inés de Castro: One, Fernando, would rule as King from 1367 to 1383 and die without a male heir. The bastard house of Aviz was the new dynasty, leading to the great age of Portuguese exploration. Inés de Castro's children by Pedro had been murdered before his death for political reasons.

5. J. E. Martínez Ferrando, *Jaime II de Aragón: Su vida familiar* (Barcelona, 1948), II, 320; one of the most pathetic letters imaginable was written by Constanza in May of this year, asking her father if he had forgotten her: *por que me avedes olvidado, o porque no es vuestra voluntat que yo guaresca deste mal . . . (idem*, p. 323).

6. He eventually entered the Order of Montesa and lived at Santas Creus. A moving exchange of correspondence would take place between Jaime II and this, his first son (Jaime), who, after turning from the path of religion to one of dissoluteness and depravity, would write later with great remorse asking his father to find out if his soul could truly be in a state of grace. The Gandesa incident, and the rumors it generated, so upset Jaime II (Giménez Soler, pp. 480–83) that he himself returned Leonor a virgin to Castile (July, 1320); after 1322 she lived at Las Huelgas, but not in the Cistercian rule (Martínez Ferrando, *Jaime II, passim*).

7. These conversations are not supported by contemporary documents; they are described at length in the *Chronicle of Alfonso XI*, Ch. 106: *BAE*, vol. 66, 240–41.

8. Strophes 1282–91 on pp. 359–61 in *El Poema de Alfonso XI*, ed. Yo Ten Cate (Madrid, 1956).

9. It is true that there will be a long, dreadful war waged in the 1350's against Aragon by Pedro I, a paranoiac who Giménez Soler believed suffered periods of insanity, and who, for example, saw fit after taking Cariñena to cut the noses from the town's male population.

While there was probably some trace of truth in Don Juan's warning to the Aragonese, the situation was not as severe as he had his envoy to Pedro IV describe it in 1345. There is extant a reply the following year from Pedro of Aragon that, while rambling on about Sardinian falcons, appears to be a coded message, impossible to decipher today (Giménez Soler, p. 646).

10. D. W. Lomax, "The Date of D. Juan Manuel's Death," *Bull. of Hispanic Studies*, XL (1963), 174.

11. A likeness of Juana may be seen in the bust on her tomb in the northeast corner of the cathedral in Toledo (Reyes Nuevos chapel).

In a chapel in the museum adjoining the Murcia cathedral, on one of the left bottom panels of a double altarpiece (top, Santa Lucía; bottom, the Virgin) painted by Barnaba da Modena, there is a small figure that is purported to be a posthumous portrait of Don Juan Manuel; it represents a bearded figure kneeling in prayer; in the Prado copy (1937) of this portrait by J. Seisdedos, Don Juan appears to be a man formerly blond or red-haired. The small figure at the bottom of a right panel is believed to be Juana Manuel.

It may be noted, incidentally, that the stunning castle with its well preserved walls and donjon dominating Peñafiel today was not where Don Juan regularly lived during his early years. During his periodic visits to Peñafiel he utilized a smaller structure, not standing today, further down the slope, to which he welcomed Sancho IV in 1294; in *Armas* he mentions continuing the construction of the castle seen today with the monarch's financial aid.

The male descendancy of the house of Manuel will end with the death of Don Juan Manuel's son Fernando, who by his wife Juana had only a daughter Blanca, who would die childless. The Manueline holdings, seized by Pedro I, were of course again in the hands of Juana Manuel after her husband became king. The two Manueles (Sancho, Enrique) mentioned in Argote's Manueline genealogy and in a number of documents and chronicles are bastard sons of Don Juan Manuel.

Chapter Three

1. The description of MS 6376 most utilized by editors is that of Eduardo Juliá, *El Conde Lucanor* (Madrid: V. Suárez, 1933), pp. xxiii-xxv. The order of Don Juan Manuel's works in this manuscript is as follows: [*Prólogo general*], *Cavallero et escudero, Armas, Castigos, Estados, El Conde Lucanor, Tratado de la Asunción, Caza.*

2. It is ironic, of course, that the very thing Don Juan feared would happen did happen, and that what remains of practically all of his works is the single error-prone copy found in MS 6376. Until very recently there has been a remarkable lack not only of universally ac-

cepted critical editions of many of the works of Don Juan Manuel, but of even moderately serviceable ones. Critics continue to this day to cite Gayangos' edition of MS 6376 (he omits *Caza*) in Vol. 51 of the *Biblioteca de Autores Españoles* (see Bibliography). A catechism of mortal sins for paleography students could be made from the ocean of accusations rained interminably on Pascual de Gayangos. Daniel Devoto's *Introducción al estudio de Don Juan Manuel y en particular de "El Conde Lucanor."* *Una Bibliografía* (Madrid: Castalia, 1972) provides a thorough description and chronology of the editions of Juan Manuel's works.

3. In his 1575 edition of *El Conde Lucanor*, Argote de Molina claimed, rightly or not, that he had seen the Peñafiel original. He also included a list of books, perhaps hastily put together, that he claimed constituted the works of Don Juan Manuel; it contains eleven titles, in addition (he says) to the *Lucanor*. In the course of listing the eleven titles, however, he (1) apparently repeats the *Lucanor* under the title *Libro de los exemplos;* (2) splits the *Libro del cavallero et del escudero* into two separate works; (3) transcribes *Engeños* as *Engaños;* and (4) as has been noted, refers to only one historical work, which he calls the *Chrónica de España.*

4. All three critics are cited in the Bibliography.

5. Edited by Baist in *Romanische Forschungen,* VII (1893), 551–56.

6. Mercedes Gaibrois de Ballesteros published his will, revealing intriguing aspects of his relations with his in-laws, in "Los testamentos inéditos de Don Juan Manuel," *Bol. Real Academia de la Historia,* XCIX (1931), 25–59; it is included among Giménez Soler's documents, as is the fascinating documentation, illuminating Don Juan's relations with his brother-in-law, the Archbishop of Toledo, published by Heinrich Finke earlier. Juan Manuel's handwriting and signature may be examined in Giménez Soler, "Un autógrafo de Don Juan Manuel," *Revue Hispanique,* XIV (1906), 606–7. A. Ballesteros Beretta's long article, "El agitado año de 1325 y un escrito desconocido de D. Juan Manuel," *Bol. Real Academia de la Historia,* CXXIV (1949), 9–58, describes the transference of authority to Alfonso XI and the exuberance of Don Juan after the mass in Valladolid that celebrated the never-consummated marriage of Alfonso XI (14 years old) and Constanza Manuel (8 or 9).

Chapter Four

1. See Aly Aben Ragel, *El libro complido en los iudizios de las estrellas,* ed. G. Hilty (Madrid: Real Academia Española, 1954), pp. xxxvii-xlii.

2. [Petrus Alfonsi], *The Scholar's Guide: A Translation of the*

Twelfth-Century "Disciplina Clericalis" of Pedro Alfonso, tr. J. R. Jones and J. E. Keller (Toronto: Pontifical Inst. of Mediaeval Studies, 1969). This English version is based on the definitive edition of A. Hilka and W. Söderhjelm (Helsinfors, 1911).

3. Even though only five manuscripts are presently extant. Four are from the fifteenth century: MSS 6376 and 4236 of the Biblioteca Nacional in Madrid and two others located in the Academia de la Historia and the Real Academia Española (see E. Juliá, cited in note 1, Chapter 3, above). The remaining manuscript is of the sixteenth century; it is MS 18415 of Biblioteca Nacional and belonged formerly to Pascual de Gayangos. (Three other MSS of the *Lucanor* in the Biblioteca Nacional in Madrid are modern copies.) The manuscript owned by the Academia Española, called the "Puñonrostro" MS (it having been possessed previously by the Count of that name), is valuable for other reasons as well: It contains the *Libro de los engaños* and the *Lucidario,* among other works.

A manuscript of the *Conde Lucanor* was apparently among the holdings of the Escorial library during the eighteenth century; its disappearance is mentioned by J. Amador de los Ríos (*Historia crítica,* IV, 470–71 [note 2]). Antonio Rodríguez-Moñino's vindication of Gallardo lists three manuscripts of the *Conde Lucanor* that were lost in the destruction of the Rightist uprising in Sevilla in 1823: one a modern copy and the other two from the fifteenth century, with one of the latter apparently the famous missing Escorial *Lucanor* (*con las armas de S. Lorenzo el Real, a cuya biblioteca perteneze*). See Rodríguez-Moñino, *Historia de una infamia bibliográfica: La de San Antonio de 1823* (Madrid: Castalia, 1965), p. 118.

Gonzalo Argote de Molina, in the "Discurso al curioso lector" in his 1575 *Conde Lucanor,* informs us that he has based this edition on three manuscripts. They cannot be identified with certainty. It is possible that he used at least one manuscript (the Escorial copy) considered lost today.

The order of the tales in the *Conde Lucanor* varies from manuscript to manuscript; even the total number of tales included varies somewhat, from the 49 of the Academia de la Historia manuscript to the 52 of the Puñonrostro copy. The order found in this study is that of MS 6376. A composite chart indicating the sequence of the tales in all five manuscripts, as well as the considerably different order utilized by Argote de Molina in his Golden Age edition, was published by Eugenio Krapf on pp. 225–26 of his edition of the Puñonrostro MS: *El Libro de Patronio o El Conde Lucanor* (Vigo, 1902). This table is reproduced on pp. xx-xxii of E. Juliá's *Conde Lucanor* (note 1, Chapter 3, above) and on pp. 296–97 of D. Devoto's *Introducción* (note 2, Chapter 3, above).

4. The *exemplo* (*enxienplo, exiemplo,* etc.) is the apologue or tale at the core of each unit; it illustrates by example the advice proffered. A tale may be called any number of things in the medieval language: *estoria, fazaña, fabliella, pastija,* etc.; it becomes an *exemplo* when used as indicated, i.e., as an organic part of the structure of an instructional lesson. The author may occasionally refer to the entire unit as an *exemplo,* even though it contains the continuing frame of dialogue as well as an *exemplo;* and the unit headings in the several MSS may be marked EXEMPLO I, etc. These uses, as well as other specific connotations in a word covering so broad a semantic area, have led to unnecessary confusion over the basic meaning of this word as employed by Juan Manuel. There are fifty-four *exemplos* in the work. Units 27 and 43 contain two each, and the author adds a final tale in the appendix. The total is 55 if Unit 3's tale-within-a-tale is counted. The Puñonrostro MS contains two additional tales seldom published; the second, on the motif "King for a Day," is incomplete. They may be read on pp. 289–92 in Knust (note 9 below) or on pp. 617–19 of Amador de los Ríos, *Historia crítica,* IV. To refer to the *exemplos* in this work as "short stories," as occasionally happens, is to be misleading, in view of the clear connotation the latter genre has come to have today. Juan Manuel does not write "short stories." The question of the lack of numerical symmetry in the works of Juan Manuel against a background of medieval insistence on the relativity of number symbolism has not been clarified to date.

5. I. R. Macpherson, *"Dios y el mundo*—the Didacticism of *El Conde Lucanor," Romance Philology,* XXIV (1970), 26–38; P. L. Barcia, *Análisis de "El Conde Lucanor"* (Buenos Aires: Centro Editor de América Latina, 1968), pp. 18–19.

6. Efforts to identify Patronio as a figure representing Don Juan Manuel's adviser and physician Salomón (of the Zag family of physicians) are made unconvincingly by Giménez Soler, p. 707. The desire to see actual events in Juan Manuel's life reflected in the episodes and characters of *Count Lucanor* is one that can be satisfied with very little imagination; such attempts are generally inconclusive. Obviously many of the questions posed by the Count can be related in a vague way to specific situations faced in the past by Juan Manuel (and faced by every other *rico-omne* as well). *Count Lucanor* is not a work of autobiography either in intent or execution. The name "Lucanor" is not a name used in medieval Castilian; possible etyma are pondered unconvincingly by A. Steiger (note 10 below) and H. Knust, "Die Etymologie des Namens *Lucanor," ZfRPh,* IX (1885), 138–40.

7. In a few units he substitutes a proverb for the couplet or supplies a quatrain or even two couplets. A bewildering final line in each unit in MS 6376 states: "And the *estoria* of this *exemplo* is as fol-

lows." Since there is a blank space following this line, Amador de los Ríos believes that the word *estoria* indicated a picture or series of drawings in an earlier, more richly decorated manuscript that is omitted in this copy, although the copyist left the blank spaces for their addition: Amador, *Historia crítica*, IV, 613–14.

8. F. Hanssen, *Notas a la versificación de Juan Manuel* (Santiago de Chile, 1902); but see M. Goyri's review in *Revista de Archivos, Bibliotecas y Museos*, VI (1902), 320. It is doubted by at least one anonymous reviewer (*Romania*, XXXII [1902], 173) that the distichs *are supposed to be lines of verse* (!).

While the major libraries on the eastern seaboard have many of the older Juan Manuel items, such as the Hanssen study above, the Gräfenberg *Cavallero et Escudero* in *Romanische Forschungen* for 1893, and the other landmark nineteenth-century editions by Baist and Knust, the Boston Public Library (since George Ticknor owned most of these books) is outstanding: the 1839 Keller *Lucanor*, the original Puybusque, York, and Eichendorff translations, the Argote princeps edition, etc.

9. M. R. Lida de Malkiel assembles a list of such collections on pp. 92–93 of her *Estudios de literatura española y comparada* (Buenos Aires: Editorial Universitaria de B. A., 1966); many are mentioned in J.-Th. Welter's *L'Exemplum dans la littérature religieuse et didactique du moyen âge* (Paris-Toulouse: Guitard, 1927) and by Knust. Hermann Knust's edition is titled *El libro de los enxiemplos del Conde Lucanor et de Patronio* (Leipzig: Dr. Seele, 1900).

The thematic index of the tales in *Count Lucanor* (and other works) in J. E. Keller, *Motif-Index of Medieval Spanish Exempla* (Knoxville: Univ. of Tenn., 1949) is incorporated into the revised edition of Stith Thompson, *Motif-Index of Folk-Literature* (Bloomington: Indiana Univ. Press, 1955–1958), 6 vols. Other basic tools in *exemplum* research are F. C. Tubach, *Index Exemplorum: A Handbook of Medieval Religious Tales*, Folklore Fellows Communications, No. 204 (Helsinki, 1969) and T. F. Crane, *The Exempla or Illustrative Stories from the "sermones vulgares" of Jacques de Vitry*, Publ. of the Folk-Lore Soc., No. 26 (London, 1890). Pages 161–98 of D. Devoto's bibliography of Don Juan Manuel are a rich and well organized source for the student tilling this terrain. S. Battaglia's two articles on the nature and evolution of the genre are basic and suggestive: "L'Esempio medievale" and "Dall'esempio alla novella," *Filologia Romanza*, VI (1959), 42–85, and VII (1960), 21–84.

10. M. R. Lida de Malkiel, *Estudios*, pp. 122–23; D. Marín draws on Lida de Malkiel, G. Moldenhauer (*Die Legende von Barlaam und Josaphat auf der iberischen Halbinsel*, [Halle: Niemayer, 1929]), and others in "El elemento oriental en D. Juan Manuel: Síntesis y revalua-

Notes and References

ción," *Comparative Literature,* VII (1955), 1–14. Note especially A. Steiger, "El Conde Lucanor," *Clavileño,* 4, 23 (1953), 1–8. Milá y Fontanals well over a century ago was already calling attention to the oriental cast of this work in his edition: *El Libro de Patronio o El Conde Lucanor* (Barcelona, 1853), pp. xv-xvi.

11. *Die Legende,* p. 81. The Barlaam legend, conveyed westward in Latin and Greek branches, tells the story of Buddha in a Christian version: A pagan prince, accompanied by a Christian tutor, discovers the meaning of old age and death after attempts are made to keep such truths from him.

Only a rare, brief mention of a possible source, parallel version, later adaptation, etc., can be given here; a full discussion would result in a book many times the size of this introduction to Don Juan Manuel (for tale 2, e.g., thirty to forty parallel versions can be easily located). In this study we are lightly scratching the surface of a large and fruitful area for study. Devoto's indications (pp. 353–464) will start the student interested in the comparative history of folk theme and artistic tale along a path rich with possibilities.

12. In seven other *exemplos* Don Juan has in mind a folk saying that usually is directly related to the story itself: Lida de Malkiel, *Estudios,* pp. 103–11.

13. "Nota sobre una fábula de D. Juan Manuel y de Juan Ruiz," accessible in the Austral (No. 190) edition of *Poesía árabe y poesía europea* (Buenos Aires: Espasa-Calpe, 1941), pp. 128–33.

14. It has been suggested that an anecdote in the *Chronicle of Alfonso X* provided Don Juan with the historical coloring that he is fond of using to touch up his bare plot (in this case, another well-known Eastern fable).

15. See especially Barcia, *Análisis,* pp. 49–61; Lida de Malkiel, *Estudios,* pp. 96–97; Knust, pp. 324–34.

16. Azorín, *Obras completas,* II (Madrid: Aguilar, 1947), pp. 1032 f; Borges' version may be read in *Antología de la literatura fantástica* (Buenos Aires: Sudamericana, n. d.), pp. 139–41, or in Vol. III of his *Obras completas* (Buenos Aires: Emecé, n. d.).

17. See E. Buceta, "La admiración de Gracián por el Inf. D. Juan Manuel," *Revista de Filología Española,* II (1924), 63–66. Gracián takes up the tale of Don Illán in unit or *agudeza* No. LVII (and three others elsewhere) in *Agudeza y arte de ingenio.*

18. The variance between this *exemplo* and the earlier version in the *Poem of Fernán González* is discussed at length in her *La idea de la fama en la edad media castellana* (México-Buenos Aires: Fondo de Cultura Económica, 1952), pp. 214–17.

19. *Orígenes de la novela,* in *Nueva Biblioteca de Autores Españoles,* I, XCI; and Lida de Malkiel, *Estudios,* p. 107.

20. But see D. Devoto, "Cuatro notas sobre la materia tradicional en Don Juan Manuel," *Bulletin Hispanique*, LXVIII (1966), 202–9.

21. Azorín, for example, wags his finger paternally at Juan Manuel in *El oasis de los clásicos* (Madrid: Bibl. Nueva, 1952), p. 27 (also in *ABC* for March 5, 1952): "What this adds up to, kind sir, is nothing less than murder . . ."

22. The usual clear dichotomy is made between the individual (the renegade may be condemned absolutely) and his station (his powers as a priest are unimpaired). Lida de Malkiel finds the miraculous leap of the host in this story similar to other tales of miracles popularized especially by the Cistercians (*Estudios*, p. 107); such incidents involving consecrated items, sacred oaths, holy relics, etc., form a body of traditional themes well known to the medieval storyteller.

23. María Rosa Lida qualifies substantially the usual remarks repeated on the Arabic origin of these tales (*Estudios*, pp. 108–9).

24. A. H. Krappe, "Le faucon de l'Infant dans *El Conde Lucanor*," *Bulletin Hispanique*, XXXV (1933), 294–97; Lida de Malkiel, *Estudios*, pp. 107–8. Krappe proposes an interpretation difficult to substantiate that involves a vindication of the author's public career. Devoto (note 20) believes No. 33 to be an essential key to understanding the author's art. Opinions vary considerably on this tale and the proper approach in relating the allegory's primary or original symbolic function with its use in the *Lucanor*.

25. *Historia de la literatura española*, I (Barcelona: G. Gili, 1946), 163–83; Valbuena insinuates that perhaps Don Juan's aversion to love (sexual) themes was due to his relationship with his mother. For a modern Asturian version of a part of this tale, see R. Menéndez Pidal, "La peregrinación de un cuento (La compra de los consejos)," *Archivum* (Oviedo), IX (1959), 13–22; this is a reprint of Don Ramón's first published (1891) research. Knust also writes at length (pp. 369–80) on this tale, but as an authority on and editor of "wisdom" literature and collections of *sententiae* his interest at this point is primarily in the selling episode.

26. An aspect of his art deftly treated by María Rosa Lida. See *Estudios*, pp. 103–11, in which this tale is briefly but incisively analyzed. A minor point is made, here and elsewhere, that Don Juan, in telling al-Hakam's story, found it convenient to omit references to the Caliph's scholarly activity. It is difficult to see why, even if he knew of this activity, he would have incorporated it into his fictional narrative; this tale, so neatly proportioned, would have lost its impact.

27. Knust has assembled with his customary diligence a barrage of references (pp. 386–96) to versions of this popular tale on the effect of malicious gossip, and to the motif of beard-cutting (the wife seeks a snip of her husband's hair for purposes of witchcraft; the husband

has been warned that his wife will kill him and so believes) that precipitates the slaughter. Sánchez Cantón (ed. *El Conde Lucanor,* 1920, p. 214) and Lida de Malkiel (*Estudios,* pp. 101–3) provide additional comment; both observe that the word *beguina* is replaced by *pelegrina* ("pilgrim") in the Puñonrostro manuscript. This tale also adds fuel to the argument over the title of the *Libro de los gatos/ cuentos;* Juan Manuel appears to use *gatos* as a term of opprobrium applied to religious hypocrites.

On the subject of heretical and semiheretical groups at this time, it may be noted that a letter in 1320 from his father-in-law to Don Juan (Giménez Soler, p. 490) mentions the routing of some leaderless, poverty-embracing fanatics (of the "pastorelli" active that year) who have crossed the Pyrenees into Aragon and murdered some Jews at Monclus in the name of Christ. Pou y Martí, Mata Carriazo, and Menéndez Pelayo have written extensively on the activity in Spain of such sects preaching primitive Christianity, new social and sexual orders, individual worship vs. the organized practices promoted by the friars, etc.

28. María Goyri de Menéndez Pidal interestingly elucidates the origins of this curious anecdote in an older version in Arabic in which the noise is frightening because it involves a superstitious belief: "Sobre el ejemplo 47 de *El Conde Lucanor,*" *Correo Erudito,* I (1940), 102–4.

29. A comparison of four versions of the theme is in K. R. Scholberg. "A Half-Friend and a Friend and a Half," *Bull. of Hispanic Studies,* XXXI (1958), 187–98; see also R. Ayerbe Chaux, "El concepto de la amistad en la obra del Inf. D. Juan Manuel," *Thesaurus,* 24 (1969), 37–49; abundant bibliography and clarification in Devoto, *Introducción,* pp. 454–59.

30. Pp. 29 ff. in Ian R. Macpherson (Note 5).

31. The psychology of suggestion is dealt with curiously in this story when the monarch, reduced to begging in the streets, and the butt of unending taunts, believes himself really a madman who thinks that he is king.

32. According to Juliá (note 1 in Chapter 3), only MS 6376 and the so-called "Gayangos" manuscript of *El Conde Lucanor* (MS 18415 in the Biblioteca Nacional in Madrid, formerly owned by Pascual de Gayangos) contain the text of these appended sections; the three remaining *Lucanor* MSS have only the first part.

33. Devoto, *Introducción,* pp. 474 ff., reproduces the solutions published by Carolina Michaëlis de Vasconcellos in 1905.

34. Many correspondences are pointed out by Knust and by Devoto (pp. 469 ff.).

35. Barcia, *Análisis,* pp. 36–42; M. Gaibrois de Ballesteros, *El*

príncipe Don Juan Manuel y su condición de escritor (Madrid: Instituto España, 1945), pp. 14–16.

Chapter Five

1. *Estudios*, pp. 94 (note), 117, 119–20.
2. See K. R. Scholberg, "Modestia y orgullo: una nota sobre D. Juan Manuel," *Hispania*, XLII (1959), 24–31; and D. Devoto, *Introducción*, pp. 280–81.
3. L. de Stefano's "La sociedad estamental en las obras de DJM," *NRFH*, XVI (1962), 329–54, takes up *Estados* and *Cavallero*, and is a synthesis of parts of a thesis on the sociology of class structure in the Castilian low Middle Ages. J. A. Maravall provides scattered comments on the topic of this thesis in 'La sociedad estamental castellana y la obra de DJM," *Cuadernos Hispanoamericanos*, 67 (Sept., 1966, 751–68. M. Torres López has two general articles on the topics of the German-Roman Empire and war in *Estados* in *Cruz y Raya*, 2 (May, 1933), 61–90, and 8 (Nov., 1933), 33–72. See especially D. Devoto, *Introducción*, pp. 258–73. An edition of *Estados* by R. B. Tate and I. R. Macpherson is now in press (Clarendon).
4. The first book was finished in May, 1330, and the dates given (for whatever they are worth) in Chapters 42 and 46 are in 1328. Constanza died in September, 1327, and it is apparent that this work was begun prior to her death, and in the course of the composition of Book I she died and John XXII conferred the Patriarchate on her brother, who quit Toledo to become archbishop of the Tarragona diocese in October, 1328. Don Juan uses the word *cunnado* (brother-in-law) twice in Book I, but not at all in Book II, in which he mentions (Chap. 45) that Juan had been Archbishop of Toledo.

"This grievously sorrowful period" of his life mentioned in Book I might have to do with Constanza's worsening condition, or to her death and that of her (and the Archbishop's) father, which occurred two months later; this was also a period of deteriorating relations with Alfonso XI over the rejection of his daughter and the child's virtual imprisonment in Toro.

5. *Estudios*, pp. 111–33.
6. I. R. Macpherson explains the semantic terrain of the word *amor* in DJM and illustrates its use in the *Lucanor* in "Amor and Don Juan Manuel," *Hispanic Review*, 39 (1971), 167–82. On the *Infinido* generally, see the Introduction in J. M. Blecua's edition (Granada, 1952).

Chapter Six

1. M. Cardenal de Iracheta demonstrates Don Juan's systematic approach in "La geografía conquense del *Libro de la caza*," *Revista de Archivos, Bibliotecas y Museos*, LIV (1948), 27–49. A general con-

sideration of the entire work is in J. M. Castro y Calvo's edition (Barcelona: C. S. I. C., 1947) based on Baist.

2. María Rosa Lida stresses the likelihood of Dominican influence on Don Juan Manuel's reasoned, intellectual approach to the doctrine: *Estudios*, p. 103. M. Gaibrois de Ballesteros posits a possible connection between Don Juan's devotion to Mary and the ceremonies celebrating the Assumption every August in Elche; the "Mystery of Elche" is thought to have medieval origins and Don Juan was master of Elche (even though the latter became part of Aragon after the treaties signed in 1304): *El príncipe D. Juan Manuel*, pp. 25–27.

3. Although Giménez Soler, in his edition and study of *Armas* (pp. 677–95), states that there is no proof that Violante hated her younger sister or that her father rejected her, he does not invalidate the mass of facts (on the Castilian royal families, the Murcia question, etc.) presented by Juan Manuel, as claimed by Lida de Malkiel (*Estudios,* p. 108 [note]).

4. A. Castro's incisive commentary on Sancho's emotional outburst as Spain's first such "literary" confession (but one whose arguments are ordered in rigorous scholastic fashion) appears in the 1954 edition of *La realidad histórica de España* (pp. 369–73), but not in the 1962 version.

Selected Bibliography

The study of Don Juan Manuel is greatly facilitated by the storehouse of well-organized information in Daniel Devoto's 505-page critical bibliography: *Introducción al estudio de Don Juan Manuel y en particular de* El Conde Lucanor. *Una Bibliografía* (Madrid: Castalia, 1972). This work is more than a bibliography of Juan Manuel: It is a substantial guide to the study, in almost every conceivable aspect, of the folktale, myth, short narrative, etc., as well as of the transmission of these genres. It also takes up in detail many of the crucial questions raised in the study of Don Juan Manuel.

The list of editions given below is selective; a complete critical chronology may be consulted in Devoto, who includes information on the nineteenth-century translations of *El Conde Lucanor:* German (Joseph Freiherrn von Eichendorff, 1840), French (Adolphe de Puybusque, 1854), and English (James York, 1868). Some forty school and popular editions of all or a substantial portion of *El Conde Lucanor* have been published in the present century.

A few titles cited in Notes and References are not repeated in the bibliography below. The reader may consult the Simón Díaz bibliography: *Bibliografía de la literatura hispánica* (Madrid: C.S.I.C., 1963), Tomo III, 1, 257–70.

PRIMARY SOURCES

Obras de Don Juan Manuel. Tomo I. Ed. José María Castro y Calvo y Martín de Riquer (Barcelona: C.S.I.C., 1955). Scholarly edition of the *Prólogo general, Libro del cavallero et del escudero, Libro de las armas,* and *Libro infinido.* This is the only volume in print of an announced "Clásicos Hispánicos" series that would have included DJM's complete works.

Crónica abreviada. Ed. Raymond L. and Mildred B. Grismer (Minneapolis: Burgess, 1958). Includes linguistic notes and *Index Verborum.* Mimeographed edition.

El Conde Lucanor. Ed. José Manuel Blecua (Madrid: Castalia, 1969). The best and most accessible edition of the version in MS 6376.

El Libro de Patronio o El Conde Lucanor. Ed. [Manuel Milá y Fontanals] (Barcelona, 1853). The nineteen-page introduction is a substantial contribution for its day. Milá includes Argote's Manueline genealogy and his "Discurso sobre la antigua poesía castellana," but states (p. v, note 1) that he was not able to consult Argote's biography of DJM until after his introduction was written.

El libro de los enxiemplos del Conde Lucanor et de Patronio. Ed. Hermann Knust (Leipzig: Dr. Seele, 1900). Prepared for publication after Knust's death by Adolf Birch-Hirschfeld; for a long time served as the standard *Lucanor* text; abundant end notes suggest a wealth of possible sources and related materials; the incomplete state of Knust's manuscript (purported to be a critical text based on MS 6376 with variants) at his death is stressed by María Goyri de Menéndez Pidal in her review in *Romania*, XXIX (1900), 600–602.

El libro de Patronio e por otro nombre El Conde Lucanor. Ed. Eugenio Krapf (Vigo, 1898). Described by the editor as based on the 1642 reprint of the Argote edition and Gayangos' edition. The order of the tales is that of Argote.

El libro de Patronio o El Conde Lucanor. Ed. Eugenio Krapf (Vigo, 1902). Based on the text of the Puñonrostro MS.

El Conde Lucanor. Ed. Francisco José Sánchez Cantón (Madrid: Saturnino Calleja, 1920). The Biblioteca Calleja edition with notes of interest; the text is that of MS 6376.

El Conde Lucanor. Ed. Eduardo Juliá (Madrid: V. Suárez, 1933). The text is that of MS 6376. The extensive introduction and its bibliography make this edition an important contribution to DJM research.

Don Juan Manuel y los cuentos medievales. Ed. María Goyri de Menéndez Pidal (Madrid: Instituto-Escuela, 1936). In the Biblioteca Literaria del Estudiante series (No. 27), and on the surface a school text, this is a scholarly edition of twenty-five of the tales, based on all five MSS. The volume includes other selections: *Calila y Dimna, Libro de los gatos, Libro de los ejemplos, Fábulas de Isopete.*

El Conde Lucanor. Ed. Pedro Henríquez Ureña (Buenos Aires: Losada, 1939). The Losada edition, long a standard text for the classroom.

El Conde Lucanor. Ed. Angel González Palencia (Zaragoza: Ebro, [1940?]). The Clásicos Ebro edition that contains twenty of the tales.

El Conde Lucanor y Patronio. Libro de los ejemplos. Ed. Federico Sainz de Robles (Madrid: Aguilar, [1945?]). The Colección Crisol edition.

Selected Bibliography

El libro de Patronio e por otro nombre El Conde Lucanor (Buenos Aires: Espasa Calpe, n.d.). The Colección Austral edition (No. 676) with the name of the editor not provided.

El Conde Lucanor. Ed. Enrique Moreno Báez (Valencia: Castalia, 1953). The Colección Odres Nuevos edition, with the medieval language modernized.

El Conde Lucanor. Ed. Juan Loveluck (Santiago de Chile: Editorial Universitaria, 1956). The Biblioteca Hispana edition, with the language modernized and with more critical apparatus than is found in the five previous popular and school editions mentioned in this list, with the exception of that of González Palencia.

Libro de los ejemplos del Conde Lucanor y de Patronio. Ed. Juan M. Lope Blanch (México: Universidad Nacional Autónoma, 1960). The Colección Nuestros Clásicos edition.

El Conde Lucanor. Ed. Amancio Bolaño e Isla (México: Porrúa, n.d.). The Sepan Cuantos . . . series edition with both medieval and modern versions.

Libro del Conde Lucanor et de Patronio. Ed. Germán Orduna (Buenos Aires, 1972). The writer has not seen this edition.

El Conde Lucanor. Ed. Ian R. Macpherson. Parallel Spanish and English selected texts, to appear in Edinburgh Bilingual Library of European Literature, published by the University of Texas.

Libro infinido y Tractado de la Asunçión. Ed. José Manuel Blecua (Granada: Universidad de Granada, 1952). Includes a long (pp. vii-xlv), informative introduction.

El Libro dela Caza. Ed. Gottfried Baist (Halle: Niemeyer, 1880). This early, immaculately prepared edition is a classic in DJM research; its 28-page study on the chronology of DJM's works is a model of clarity.

Libro de la caza. Ed. José María Castro y Calvo (Barcelona: C.S.I.C., 1947). The text and notes are based on Baist's edition; includes a rambling, uneven 77-page study on the sport of falconry, falconry in literature, etc.

Libro de los estados. Ed. José María Castro y Calvo (Barcelona: F. I. U. [Departamento de Literatura, Universidad de Barcelona], 1968). Numerous errors left uncorrected in the printing. No critical apparatus.

Libro de los estados. Ed. Robert B. Tate and Ian R. Macpherson. To be published by Oxford University Press, 1973.

[*Obras de D. Juan Manuel*] in *Biblioteca de Autores Españoles,* vol. 51 (titled *Escritores en prosa anteriores al siglo XV*). Ed. Pascual de Gayangos (Madrid, 1860). Does not include *Caza* or *Crónica abreviada* and is first edition of all of DJM's works except the *Lucanor.*

Antología. Ed. Manuel Cardenal de Iracheta ([Madrid]: Ediciones Fe, 1942). Selections from DJM's works (especially those not so well known) arranged by theme: *La obra de Dios, El mundo moral, Arte militar,* etc. Includes Argote's biography of DJM and his vocabulary.

Note 1: Two manuscripts of *El Conde Lucanor* have been edited in unpublished doctoral dissertations: the MS of the Academia de la Historia (Rigo Mignani, University of Washington, Seattle, 1957) and MS 4236 of the Biblioteca Nacional in Madrid (Nydia Rivera Gloeckner, Pennsylvania State University, University Park, 1971).

Note 2: James York's English translation, *Count Lucanor or, the Fifty Pleasant Stories of Patronio* (Westminster, 1868), has been reprinted from time to time (latest: a handsomely bound, privately subsidized edition of one thousand copies in Alhambra, California, 1953). The physician York is criticized by E. Juliá (ed. *El Conde Lucanor,* 1933, p. xxxvi) for knowing (*lege:* using) Puybusque's French translation and described as quite deficient in his knowledge of Spanish. These judgments may be a bit severe. An adaptation of *Count Lucanor* (Dial Press, 1970) for six-to-ten-year-olds (?), described as the first English translation of this work, is reviewed in *The New York Times Book Review* for November 8, 1970.

SECONDARY SOURCES

ALBORG, JUAN LUIS. *Historia de la literatura española. Edad Media y Renacimiento,* I (Madrid: Gredos, 1966). General information on Don Juan Manuel on pages 153–65.

AMADOR DE LOS RIOS, JOSE. *Historia crítica de la literatura española* (Madrid, 1863), IV, 205–300. A sound and substantial presentation by a careful, brilliant scholar who may have been too much so for his age (and later ages as well). His century-old pages on Don Juan Manuel that break ground are seldom surpassed in later literary histories.

AYERBE CHAUX, REINALDO. "El concepto de la amistad en la obra del Infante Don Juan Manuel," *Thesaurus,* XXIV (1969), 37–49.

AZORIN. *Obras completas,* II (Madrid: Aguilar, 1947). The word portraits and paraphrases of DJM and some of his passages (tales 5, 11, 39, 41, etc.) are on pages 1032–53.

BALLESTEROS BERETTA, ANTONIO. "El agitado año de 1325 y un escrito desconocido de Don Juan Manuel," *Bol. Real Academia de la Historia,* CXXIV (1949), 9–58. The document by DJM traces his genealogy. This study illuminates in depth the political crisis at this point in Castilian history.

————. "Un documento de Don Juan Manuel," *Correo Erudito*, II (1941), 268–72. The document (March, 1321) provides for an annual gift of salt to the Guadalajara convent of Santa Clara.

BARCIA, PEDRO L. *Análisis de* El Conde Lucanor (Buenos Aires: Centro Editor de América Latina, 1968). A 64-page introduction that presents facts lucidly, with a twelve-page study of Exemplo XI.

BATTAGLIA, SALVATORE. "Dall'esempio alla novella," *Filologia Romanza*, VII (1960), 21–84. On the relationship of *exemplum* and artistic tale, with mention of DJM.

BUCETA, ERASMO. "La admiración de Gracián por el Infante Don Juan Manuel," *Revista de Filología Española*, XI (1924), 63–66. Calls attention to the passages in *Agudeza y arte de ingenio*.

CALDERA, ERMANNO. "Retorica, narrativa e didattica nel *Conde Lucanor*," *Miscellanea di Studi Ispanici*, XIV (1966), 5–120. Views the *CL* from many perspectives: style, organization, reflection of *Estados*, evolution of narrative art, etc.

CANELLAS LOPEZ ANGEL. "Datos para la historia de los reinos peninsulares en el primer tercio del siglo XIV. Dieciocho neuvos documentos de la alacena de Zurita," *Bol. de la Real Academia de la Historia*, 145 (1959), 231–86. Some of the incidents treated deeply involve Juan Manuel.

CARDENAL DE IRACHETA, MANUEL. "La geografía conquense del *Libro de la caza*," *Revista de Archivos, Bibliotecas, y Museos*, LIV (1948), 27–49. The excellent map requires a magnifying glass.

CASTRO, AMERICO. *La realidad histórica de España* (México: Porrúa, 1965). Segunda edición renovada. Occasional references to DJM: DJ's views on the Reconquest, Semitic presence in Castile, etc.

CASTRO Y CALVO, JOSE MARIA. *El arte de gobernar en las obras de Don Juan Manuel* (Barcelona: C.S.I.C.-Inst. Antonio de Nebrija, 1945). Traces previous critical opinion on DJM, catalogues presumed statements on the "education of princes" theme, etc.; curiously titled.

DE STEFANO, LUCIANA. "La sociedad estamental en las obras de Don Juan Manuel," *Nueva Revista de Filología Hispánica*, XVI (1962), 329–54. On the structure of society and social classes.

DEVOTO, DANIEL. "Cuatro notas sobre la materia tradicional en Don Juan Manuel," *Bulletin Hispanique*, LXVIII (1966), 187–215. Takes up the "General Prologue" and tales 3, 25, and 33 in the *Lucanor*.

DEYERMOND, A. D. *A Literary History of Spain. The Middle Ages* (London and New York: Ernest Benn-Barnes and Noble, 1971). The most accurate information in manual form.

DI STEFANO, GIUSEPPE. "Don Juan Manuel nel suo *Libro de la caza*,"

Quaderni Ibero-Americani, 31 (1965), 379–90. General and pertinent observations on the book on falconry.

DODDIS MIRANDA, A. and SEPULVEDA DURAN, G. *Estudios sobre Juan Manuel* (Santiago de Chile: Edit. Universitaria, 1957). 2 vols. Mimeograph copy of twenty items: previously published articles, studies extracted from editions, etc.

DON JUAN MANUEL STUDIES. Ed. I. R. Macpherson and R. B. Tate. To be published by Tamesis Press, with articles by J. P. England, K. R. Scholberg, J. Valdeón Baruque, Salvador de Moxó, G. Orduna, and the editors.

ESQUER TORRES, RAMON. "Dos rasgos estilísticos en Don Juan Manuel," *Revista de Filología Española,* XLVII (1964), 429–35. On repetitive nature of Juan Manuel's prose.

GAIBROIS DE BALLESTEROS, MERCEDES. *El príncipe don Juan Manuel y su condición de escritor* (Madrid: Publ. del Inst. de España, 1945). A 31-page public lecture on Juan Manuel's general qualities as a writer, with flattering remarks that may be counterpoised to her harsh criticisms of him in her *María de Molina* and elsewhere.

———. "Los testamentos inéditos de Don Juan Manuel," *Bol. Real Academia de la Historia,* XCIX (1931), 25–59. The second of the two wills (1339, 1340) reveals interesting personal antagonisms.

GIMENEZ SOLER, ANDRES. *Don Juan Manuel. Biografía y estudio crítico* (Zaragoza, 1932). This large volume, written prior to 1906, contains a biography (which will stand until the definitive one is written), a study of DJM's works (with emphasis on what they reveal of their author), and a rich collection of 591 documents, plus other previously published materials related to DJM's life and times. A review critical of the editing of this work is in *RFE,* XX (1933), 185–187.

———. "Un autógrafo de Don Juan Manuel," *Revue Hispanique,* XIV (1906), 606–7. Includes facsimile of a 24-line letter written by DJM himself to Alfonso IV of Aragon, apparently in 1332.

GOYRI DE MENENDEZ PIDAL, MARIA. "Sobre el ejemplo 47 de *El Conde Lucanor,*" *Correo Erudito,* I (1940), 102–4. Explains the superstitious belief that in turn explains the fear of the *mora medrosa.*

HANSSEN, FEDERICO. "Notas a la versificación de Juan Manuel," *Anales de la Universidad de Chile,* CIX (1901), 539–63. The reprint of this article is mentioned in note 8, Chapter 4.

HEER, FRIEDRICH. *The Medieval World: Europe 1100–1350* (New York: New American Library, 1962?). A Mentor Book. Highly readable, authoritative social, intellectual, etc., history.

HUERTA TEJADAS,FELIX. *Vocabulario de las obras de Don Juan Ma-*

Selected Bibliography

nuel (Madrid, 1956). Separata del *BRAE*. This reprint combines sections previously published in Vols. 34–36 of *Boletín de la Real Academia Española* (1954–1956). Its final section contains a summary-analysis of DJM's works, editions, etc.

ISOLA, DELIA L. "Las instituciones en la obra de D. Juan Manuel," *Cuadernos de Historia de España*, 21–22 (1954), 70–145. General review of social and political ideas in *Estados*, etc.

JACKSON, GABRIEL. *The Making of Medieval Spain* (New York: Harcourt Brace Jovanovich, 1972). General historical survey and facts.

KINKADE, RICHARD P. "Sancho IV: Puente literario entre Alfonso el Sabio y Juan Manuel," *PMLA*, 87 (1972), 1039–51.

KRAPPE, ALEXANDER H. "Le faucon de l'Infant dans *El Conde Lucanor*," *Bulletin Hispanique*, XXXV (1933), 294–97. On the moral of tale 33 in the *Lucanor*.

LAZARO CARRETER, FERNANDO. "Don Juan Manuel, creador de la prosa castellana," to appear in *Anuario de Estudios Medievales* (Barcelona, 1972–1973).

LIDA DE MALKIEL, MARIA ROSA. "Tres notas sobre Don Juan Manuel," *Romance Philology*, IV (1950–1951), 155–94. Reprinted in her *Estudios de literatura española y comparada* (Buenos Aires, 1966), pp. 92–133. Incisive commentary on Dominican, classical, etc., influences, use of proverbs, etc.

———. *La idea de la fama en la edad media castellana* (México-Buenos Aires: Fondo de Cultura Económica, 1952). Underscores succinctly differences in attitude in Don Juan Manuel and other medieval writers, etc.

LOMAX, DEREK W. "The Date of Don Juan Manuel's Death," *Bulletin of Hispanic Studies*, XL (1963), 174. DJM's name ("domnus Iohannes de Uillena filius infantis Manuelis") and the date (June 13, 1348) appear on a list of deceased benefactors and members of the Order of Santiago.

LOPEZ ESTRADA, FRANCISCO. *Introducción a la literatura medieval española* (Madrid: Gredos, 1970). Tercera edición renovada. Orientation to medieval period, genres, etc.

MACPHERSON, IAN R. "Don Juan Manuel: The Literary Process," to appear in *Studies in Philology*, LXX (1973).

———. "*Dios y el mundo*–the Didacticism of *El Conde Lucanor*," *Romance Philology*, XXIV (1970), 26–38. Examines the contradiction in moralizing aim and worldly advice in the *CL*.

———. "*Amor* and Don Juan Manuel," *Hispanic Review*, 39 (1971), 167–82. On the meaning and uses of this word (and concept).

MARAVALL, JOSE A. "La sociedad estamental castellana y la obra de Don Juan Manuel," *Cuadernos Hispanoamericanos*, 67 (1966),

751–68. A review article on L. de Stefano's work (see above). Accessible also in Maravall's *Estudios de historia del pensamiento español* (Madrid, 1967), which contains other items of interest to students of DJM.

MENENDEZ PELAYO, MARCELINO. *Orígenes de la novela*, I (Madrid, 1905). In *Nueva Biblioteca de Autores Españoles*, I, lxxxvi-xcv. The insights and opinions on these pages of general criticism have had widespread influence.

MENENDEZ PIDAL, RAMON. "Nota sobre una fábula de don Juan Manuel y de Juan Ruiz," in *Poesía árabe y poesía europea* (Buenos Aires: Espasa-Calpe, 1941). Colección Austral (No. 190). On tale 5 in *Conde Lucanor*.

MILLE Y GIMENEZ, JUAN. "La fábula de la lechera al través de las diversas literaturas," in his *Estudios de literatura española* (La Plata: Univ. de La Plata, 1928), pp. 1–32. Published as Tomo VII of Biblioteca Humanidades (Univ. de La Plata). One page in this sketch of the milkmaid story is devoted to Juan Manuel and contains a summary of *exemplo 7* in the *Lucanor*.

MONTGOMERY, THOMAS. "Don Juan Manuel's Tale of Don Illán and its Revision by Jorge Luis Borges," *Hispania*, XLVII (1964), 464–66.

NYKL, ALOIS R. "Arabic Phrases in *El Conde Lucanor*," *Hispanic Review*, X (1942), 12–17. Another transcription to add to the list of interpretations of DJM's Arabic sentences.

ORDUNA, GERMAN. "Los prólogos a la *Crónica abreviada* y al *Libro de la caza*. La tradición alfonsí y la primera época en la obra literaria de don Juan Manuel," to appear in *Cuadernos de Historia de España* (1973). Will include an edition of the first of the two prologues.

———. "¿Un catálogo más de obras de don Juan Manuel?" to appear in *Bull. of Hispanic Studies* (1973).

———. "'Fablar complido' y 'Fablar breve et escuro': Procedencia oriental de esta disyuntiva en la obra literaria de don Juan Manuel." To appear in *Homenaje a Fernando Antonio Martínez*, to be published by the Instituto Caro y Cuervo (Bogotá).

PUIBUSQUE, ADOLPHE DE. *Le comte Lucanor. Apologues et fabliaux du XIVe siècle* (Paris: Amyot, 1854). This translation's 160-page introduction on DJM's life and works merits mention as a noteworthy, substantial contribution in its day.

RUFFINI, MARIO. "Les sources de Don Juan Manuel," *Les Lettres Romanes*, VII (1953), 27–49. Rambles on in a general way about Llull, *Barlaam*, Arabic sources, books on falconry, etc. Apparently has not seen the Knust *Lucanor*.

SANCHEZ ALBORNOZ, CLAUDIO. *España. Un enigma histórico* (Buenos

Selected Bibliography

Aires: Editorial Sudamericana, 1971). Tercera edición. 2 tomos. Numerous references to Don Juan Manuel as writer and political figure throughout both volumes.

SANCHEZ CANTON, F. J. "Cinco notas sobre Don Juan Manuel," *Correo Erudito,* I (1940), 63–64. Biographical and historical points of interest.

SCHOLBERG, KENNETH R. "Juan Manuel, personaje y autocrítico," *Hispania,* XLIV (1961), 457–60. On DJM's innovative manner of introducing self in works in third person.

————. "Sobre el estilo del *Conde Lucanor,*" *Kentucky Foreign Language Quarterly,* X (1963), 198–203.

————. "Modestia y orgullo: una nota sobre Don Juan Manuel," *Hispania,* XLII (1959), 24–31.

————. "A Half-Friend and a Friend and a Half," *Bull. of Hispanic Studies,* XXXV (1958), 187–98. A comparative study, taking up tale 48 in *Conde Lucanor.*

STEIGER, A. "El Conde Lucanor," *Clavileño,* 4, 23 (1953), 1–8. Meandering commentary spiced with occasional sharp insights.

STURM, HARLAN. "The *Conde Lucanor:* The First *Exemplo,*" *Modern Language Notes,* 84 (1969), 286–92. In its relationship to rest of work.

TAMAYO, JUAN ANTONIO. "Escritores didácticos de los siglos XIII y XIV," in *Historia general de las literaturas hispánicas,* ed. G. Díaz-Plaja (Barcelona: Barna, 1949), Vol. I. General information on Don Juan Manuel on pages 459–66.

TORRES LOPEZ, MANUEL. "El arte y la justicia de la guerra en el *L. de los estados* de Don Juan Manuel," *Cruz y Raya,* 8 (1933), 33–72. General exposition of DJM's views on these topics.

————. "La idea del imperio en el *L. de los estados* de D. Juan Manuel," *Cruz y Raya,* 2 (1933), 61–90. On the awareness in Castile of the Empire and its internal conflicts, etc.

VALBUENA PRAT, ANGEL. *Historia de la literatura española,* I (Barcelona: G. Gili, 1946). General treatment of DJM on pages 163–83.

VALLEJO, JOSE. "Sobre un aspecto estilístico de don Juan Manuel: Notas para la historia de la sintaxis española," in *Homenaje ofrecido a Menéndez Pidal* (Madrid, 1925), II, 63–85. Suggests that DJM sought to eliminate archaic expressions (*maguer que, pero que*).

VARVARO, ALBERTO. "La Cornice del *Conde Lucanor,*" in *Studi di letteratura spagnuola* (Roma: Univ. di Roma, 1964), pp. 187–95. Analyzes use of frame in this work.

VELASCO Y ARIAS, MARIA. *"El Conde Lucanor" y sus mujeres* (Buenos Aires, 1935). A 150-page book, strongly feminist, but inconclusive on the psychology of female types in the *Lucanor* (*la posesa, la madre cariñosa,* etc.).

WELTER, J.-TH. *L*'Exemplum dans la littérature religieuse et didactique du moyen âge (Paris-Toulouse: Guitard, 1927). Basic study of *exemplum* and its place in medieval literature.

Index

[157]

Index

Index

DATE DUE

GAYLORD   PRINTED IN U.S.A